NYPD

NYPD

**On the streets with the
New York City
Police Department's
Emergency Service Unit**

Samuel M. Katz

Windrow & Greene

© Samuel M. Katz 1995

This edition published in Great Britain 1995 by
Windrow & Greene Ltd.
5 Gerrard Street,
London W1V 7LJ

Designed by Ian Penberthy
Printed in Spain

A CIP catalogue record for this book is available from the
British Library

ISBN 1 85915 042 X

Contents

Preface

This book had its genesis in the winter of 1993. After writing on the Middle East, terrorism, the Israel Defense Forces, American and European special forces and other related material for nearly six years, following units in Israel, southern Lebanon, Great Britain and Germany, I felt it was time to cover something closer to home. As a native New Yorker who has spent most of his 32 years in the five boroughs, my choice for a new focus was clear. I had wanted to write an article on the New York City Police Department for some time; and being interested in counter-terrorist and hostage-rescue units, I was naturally drawn to the department's elite Emergency Service Unit (ESU).

I was commissioned by the British edition of *Penthouse* to write the piece; and before I even knew the difference between a "pin job" and a "perp search", I contacted the office of the NYPD's Deputy Commissioner for Public Information. They instructed me to contact the Special Operations Division in Flushing Meadows, Queens, in order to arrange my ride-along and my contact. Not knowing what to expect, I ventured to the grounds of the World's Fair Press Building, the SOD and ESU headquarters, where I signed a waiver relieving the NYPD of all legal responsibility should I get myself shot, torched or thrown off a building; and was issued with a bullet-proof vest and a cup of coffee. The man who was to take me out into the field that day was one Lieutenant Bob Sobocienski.

Lieutenant "Sobo" was an impressive and friendly figure even at first sight; I was immediately struck by the chestful of medal ribbons worn above his gold lieutenant's badge. The more I got to know, the more impressed I became. With 26 years on the job and unrivaled anti-crime experience and intuition, he is one of the nicest people anyone could have the privilege to meet. I couldn't have been luckier in having Lt.Sobocienski as my personal guide through the history and day-to-day life of the NYPD's Emergency Service Unit.

Eventually, my article on ESU was published by some fourteen magazines in as many countries around the world. Over the course of time, following visits to Floyd Bennet Field and return ride-alongs, Lt.Sobocienski became my "rabbi" in the unit, the man to teach me the ropes and to ensure that I was "taken care of." When I received the DCPI's authorization for

Above Inspector John Harkins (center), commander of the NYPD's Emergency Service Unit.

this book he was kind enough to volunteer to be my guide. Over the course of nearly eight months I was fortunate to ride along with Lt.Sobocienski on jobs throughout the city - from "hits" to cop shootings, from barricaded EDPs to "pin jobs". He introduced me to the officers as an honorary member of the ESU family, and always made sure that I was looked after just right. This book would not have been possible without Lt.Sobocienski's kindness and generosity, and I am forever grateful for his efforts on my behalf - I couldn't have met a finer cop or made a better friend.

In the course of writing this book I would learn that most officers in ESU were remarkably friendly and helpful. In the various "Trucks" of the unit I have met some of the most dedicated professionals in the world. Although room was scarce inside the cabin of an REP, between the radios, the clipboards, and the 12-gauge Ithaca mounted on the floor, the officers asked to let me ride along with them gladly tucked in their guts and, with a smile and a joke, allowed me along for a tour. They always made sure I was kept informed, and always seemed glad to pour an extra cup of coffee, and invite me over to quarters for some of the most fabulous meals to be found in the city. Whenever, on a job, the sight of such an obvious civilian sparked

Above Lieutenant Bob Sobocienski, one of the ESU's City North Supervisors, against the Lower Manhattan skyline. His patient assistance and advice to the author at every stage of this project have been invaluable.

Below Captain Ralph Pascullo, former commander of the Housing Police's Emergency Rescue Unit and now an ESU patrol captain, monitors the SOD radio on a rooftop of the Alfred Smith Housing Project overlooking the Brooklyn Bridge (which he climbed while in STS).

the curiosity of a precinct sergeant, an ESU officer would immediately put a hand on my shoulder and say, "It's OK, he's with us." No five words could have been more reassuring. Spending time with the unit on a weekly basis became a privilege rather than work, and has been among the most rewarding experiences of my life.

If space allowed, I would like to thank individually the 350 men and women of ESU; and I have tried, in the following pages, to include as many as possible in the narrative and accompanying photographs. I would like to thank first of all Inspector John Harkins, the ESU commanding officer, for his kind support of this project. I would also like to offer warm thanks to Captains Tom Martin and Curt Wargo for their kind help and support, as well as Captain Ralph Pasculло. Special thanks are due to Lieutenants Tom Stokes and George Shanley, as well as to Lieutenant Ray Butkiewicz (whose son, Officer Ray Butkiewicz Jr., is now serving in ESU at Seven-Truck.) I must also record my gratitude to Sergeants Eugene O'Connor and Karl Smith, One-Truck; Lieutenant Owen McCaffrey, and Sergeants Juan Garcia and Patrick Murphy of Two-Truck; Sergeant Charles Girven of Three-Truck; Sergeant John Coughlin of Four-Truck; Lieutenant Mary Zaleski and Sergeant Tom Sullivan of Five-Truck; Sergeant Jack Cambria of Six-Truck; Sergeant Marty Garvey of Eight-Truck; Sergeant John Boesch of Nine-Truck; and Sergeant Paul Hargrove of Ten-Truck.

My special thanks must go to Lieutenants Mike Libretto and Richard Greene who, together with Lieutenant Sobocienski, are known as the "Three Amigos" during their simultaneous shifts supervising various parts of the city. Each lieutenant had his own style of work, his own viewpoints of command and of the job; each was incredibly generous with his time and insights, and both charismatic and impressive to watch in the field. Special thanks for their kindness and patience are also due to Detective Denis Burke and Police Officer Kris Brandt at Floyd Bennet Field. After having seen Israeli, British and German GSG-9 tactical instructors at work, I can confirm that these officers are as experienced and knowledgeable as the best in the world.

I am also happy to record my gratitude to PO Dan Donnelly, PO Seth Gahr, PO James McVey, Detective Henry Medina, PO John Politoski, PO Peter Conlin, PO Peter Tetukevich, PO John D'Allara, PO Vincent Martinez, PO Auggie Ameleto, and PO Edward H.D'Alessandro of Two-Truck, and PO Mike Corr, for their time in Upper Manhattan; PO Billy Johnson and PO Dan Reilly of Ten-Truck for a memorable 12-to-8 in Queens; PO Jim Helliesen, PO Carl Russo and PO Tony Mangiarcina for their lesson on Brooklyn South; Eight-Truck squad members PO Winston Smith, PO Dave Kayen, PO Bill Pieszak, and Detective Tony Sanpietro for sharing philosophical lessons on life and police work; Detective James Romagnoli from Nine-Truck; PO Glenn Klein and PO Ron Harris of Ten-Truck; PO Robert Johnson, PO Tom Flannery and PO Steven J.Lanoce of Four-Truck; PO Frank Camastro, PO Ed Foley and PO Al Rosenthal for their instruction on the Bronx's most memorable areas and moments. Thanks are also due to PO Tony Anderson, PO Tito Perez, PO Alex Cingone, and PO Brian Gregory for their help with the A-Team; PO Dennis O'Connell at Floyd Bennet Field; PO Renee Davy, PO Tim Wolf and Detective Dave Hayes at ESU; and PO Ken LeGrow at the Rodmen's Neck range.

Because of all these "good people," I was afforded the chance to see and do things that few people in this city - even cops - ever get to do, and I will always be grateful.

Finally, I would like to thank former DCPI John Miller for his involvement in this project and his office's kind support. For years, the NYPD was a closed society - especially to journalists and writers. The office thought that any coverage by the city's "venomous" press could only be bad, and a trench warfare mentality set in among the officers in the field and the bosses who commanded them. Everything was always so politically charged, in the city and in the department, that officers were routinely ordered to make "no comment" even when it was evidently important for their story to be told. Some public information officers simply hoped that their phones wouldn't ring with any more contentious question than the proper spelling of a crime victim's name, or the wording of some anodyne quote from a chief or deputy inspector.

When Police Commissioner William Bratton took over the helm of the NYPD in January 1994 he vowed to re-invent the department, and one of his first orders of business was to hire John Miller - a successful television reporter covering mobsters and City Hall - as the new Deputy Commissioner for Public Information. Taking a $500,000 pay cut, Mr.Miller accepted the challenge; and immediately revitalized the office into an information superhighway for writers, journalists and film crews eager to work with the NYPD. He understood that the negative press the NYPD sometimes received stemmed from the lack of any infrastructure to enable officers to tell their side of the story.

Soon, film crews began riding along with the NYPD, including those from the television series *"Cops"*; and the NYPD earned such dividends in popularity and respect that even significant corruption scandals failed to make the front pages of the city tabloids. Seeing the police on the nightly news in a positive light reassured the city's inhabitants that something was actually being done about crime - that the city was actually getting better. Since crime is as much a matter of public perception as actual statistics, New Yorkers had never felt better about their police department. DCPI Miller was often out on the street for sixteen hours a day in his patrol car, seeking "jobs" that might spark media interest. He was on hand for every job in every borough. His efforts were a tremendous boost for the morale of the officers in the department, and DCPI Miller and company will surely be missed.

I would like to dedicate this book to the ESU officers who have fallen in the line of duty; and to those who "suit up" every day to keep the streets of the city safe. They are undoubtedly New York's Finest, and the nation's as well. Stay safe, guys.

Samuel M. Katz
April 1995

Above In quarters: Two-Truck officers carry out routine chores during a rare quiet evening.

Below Three-Truck's "Adam car" responds to an EDP call in the confines of the 41st Precinct - better known as "Fort Apache".

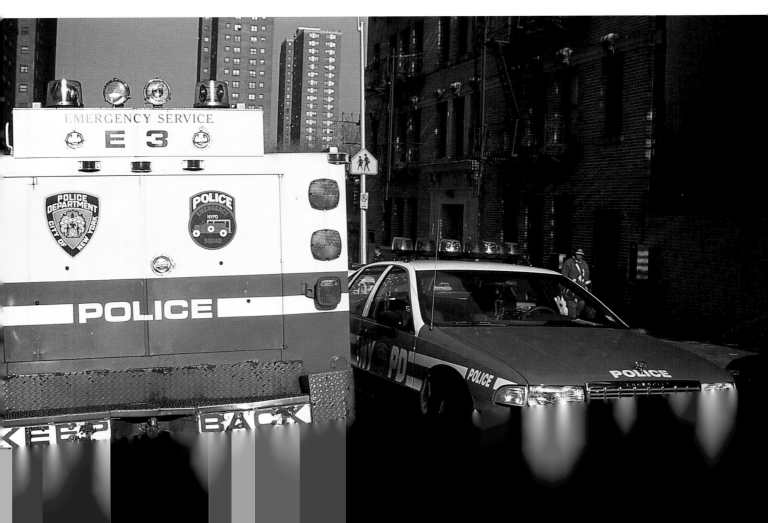

Glossary

In order to avoid scattering the narrative too thickly with quote marks and explanatory footnotes, there follows a brief, selectively expurgated, definitely unofficial and entirely unauthorized glossary of NYPD and ESU vernacular terms which may be encountered in the text:

Boss - Term for senior officers, from lieutenant (in certain units) to captain, deputy inspector, inspector, and commissioner.

Bus - Ambulance

Camel stop - An unauthorized taxi stand where unlicensed livery cab drivers congregate; usually this will be in a "no parking" and "no standing" zone.

CCRB - Civilian Complaint Review Board; the body before which, in ESU legend, an officer may find him or her self when a "perp", eager to sue the city, claims to have had, e.g., his leg bitten off in the course of being arrested.

Central - Central Despatch

Chauffeur - Driver of an ESU truck

CSU - Crime Scene Unit

DeeWee - The phonetic term for DWI, Driving While Intoxicated - a habit that all too often results in a "pin job".

DT - Street-slang for Detective

EDP - Emotionally Disturbed Person; known years ago by the less politically correct term "psycho".

EMS - New York City's Emergency Medical Service of para-medics, who administer emergency medical care to tens of thousands of people each year throughout the five boroughs. Because EMS technicians are overworked, poorly paid and often unappreciated by the general public, "EMS" has also come to stand for "Every Minute Sucks."

FAT - NYPD's Fugitive Apprehension Team

Below "Truck"

Feds - Federal law enforcement agencies, which sometimes work with the NYPD and ESU, e.g. the FBI, DEA, Secret Service and US Marshals Service.

Field, The - ESU equipment storage and tactical training facility at Floyd Bennet Field, Brooklyn.

Five-0 - Police (at least they are paying attention to the TV culture...)

Flying - "To fly" is the NYPD term for leaving the confines of ones usual Precinct or Truck to fill in for a shortage of manpower in another location.

Fort Hair Spray - Unofficial NYPD nickname for the 62nd Precinct in Bensonhurst, made famous in the film "Saturday Night Fever."

Fort Surrender - Unofficial NYPD nickname for the 66th Precinct in Williamsburg, routinely overrun, without resistance, by disgruntled Hasidic Jews complaining about one thing or another.

Above "Good people"

Go down, to - To get arrested

Good people - All-purpose NYPD compliment meaning "kosher", nice, reliable, friendly, hard working, etc., irrespective of race, religion or sexual orientation.

Gun run - Search for a weapon reported sighted in the hands of a "perp".

HAZMAT - Acronym for Hazardous Material

Hit - Tactical assault on a criminal location.

Hole in the Donut - The affluent enclave of Columbia University, surrounded by Harlem.

Job - A specific task or mission to which ESU officers are called; also, "on the job", meaning "in NYPD service", as e.g. "I've been on the job for five years."

MOS - Member of the Service, or police officer - an acronym used on divisional radios.

Mope - Unauthorized NYPD term for "perp"

Mutt - Unauthorized NYPD term for "perp"

OC - Organized crime

One PP - 1 Police Plaza, NYPD headquarters and 911 nerve-center, located in downtown Manhattan near the mayor's office at City Hall.

Open carrier - Police officer or vehicle with an open radio.

Package - An escorted prisoner or VIP

Paying the rent - For police officers, the handing out of a certain number of traffic summonses and moving violations.

Perp - Perpetrator, criminal

Pin job - Extrication of trapped auto accident casualties

Pull the pin, to - To retire

Above "Perp"

Puppy - Pitbull (also, "quiet puppy" - a pitbull with its voice box surgically removed.)

Puzzle Palace - Police officer's term for 1 Police Plaza

Rabbi - An individual's guide and guardian angel in the department.

Rat Squad - Officers and detectives assigned to IAB, Internal Affairs Bureau.

Red Menace - Strictly unofficial term for the New York City Fire Department (also "Rubbermen", term of affection and respect for members of that magnificent organisation.)

REP - Radio Emergency Patrol, the smaller of the vehicles regularly operated by ESU "Trucks".

Rip - A loss of pay due to a disciplinary infraction, e.g. unauthorized moonlighting.

RMP - Radio Mobile Patrol, the NYPD blue and white sector car.

Skel - Homeless vagrant

Soboisms - Certain vernacular terms and expressions unique to Lt.Bob Sobocienski.

SNAG - Special Narcotics and Guns Unit

SNEU - Special Narcotics Enforcement Unit

SOD - Special Operations Division

TARU - Technical and Research Unit

Truck - Where spelt with a capital "T" in this book, one of the city's ten regional ESU squads, or the squad's quarters; with a lower-case "t", the squad's heavy vehicle carrying the full range of emergency equipment.

Tunnel Rats - New York City Transit (subway) cops

White Shirts - The term for bosses above the rank of lieutenant, who all wear white shirts on the job.

Below "MOS"

1

"Anytime, Anywhere, Any Place": An ESU Overview

"I don't want to be thanked by the citizens I help or even by the cops I back up. It is me who should thank them, and the city, for letting me be where I am and do the job that I do."

ESU Detective Tony Sanpietro, Eight-Truck.

It was a typical winter's morning for the New York City Police Department's Emergency Service Unit, and the E-Men were on the job. The 8-4 shift had barely had the chance to drink a cup of coffee and look at the headlines before the radio started summoning them from throughout the northern half of the island. At around noon Two-Truck's "Adam" and "Boy" cars, together with the "truck", were about to head back to quarters to grab a meal when the SOD radio called them to a division assignment in Harlem's notorious 32nd Precinct. A division assignment meant only one thing: a "hit".

The New York City Housing Authority was reclaiming a building on 145th Street and Adam Clayton Powell Boulevard, and needed the police to remove squatters, crack dealers and gun sellers who had nested in the four-storey walk-up. The cops, realizing the potential for violence, called in ESU: after all, they are the cop's back-up. For this hit, however, even ESU needed back-up: nine apartments were to be entered, and the six men of Two-Truck weren't enough. Several officers were "flown" from Ten-Truck in northern Queens, and all of Four-Truck from the Bronx were invited to participate in the raid.

Inside the "3-2's" Operations Room a dozen precinct officers sat for the briefing, along with three plain-clothes officers and the twelve Emergency Service cops. The female sergeant commanding the show had ten years on the job and was fourth generation Irish NYPD. An experienced Harlem cop, she knew that her officers would simply secure the outside of the building, the alley and the roof. It would be ESU who would be breaking down the doors and cuffing the perps; and the sergeant handed the show to the ESU City North Supervisor (CNS), Lieutenant Mike Libretto, a 23-year veteran of the force who had started out as a foot cop in the "3-2" when Harlem was ablaze with tenement fires and cop killings. Against the background noises of suspects being brought to the front desk for booking, the officers briefly studied a blueprint of the building; but these guys had done so many hits that charts and maps meant little to them. All they needed were two pieces of information: a look at the faces of the plain-clothes officers they would find inside the building; and who was driving the H-Car - the police car assigned to rush any wounded officer to hospital.

The briefing was short and to the point. Lt.Libretto told the regular cops not to be alarmed if they heard loud explosions - these would be the diversionary devices that ESU occasionally uses when gaining entry to a location with known perpetrators. The officers were told that they should seize anyone caught around the building, since chances were that they were dirty. With the briefing details wrapped, the ESU cops stubbed their cigarettes and headed outside to 135th Street and their waiting REPs and trucks, where they suited-up under the curious gaze of passing bus passengers, car drivers and onlookers.

Heavy Kevlar ballistic vests with built-in pouches were strapped on, and Kevlar "Fritz" helmets. Each officer grabbed either a German-made Heckler & Koch MP5

Left PO Dave Kayen, Eight-Truck, confers with precinct cops in Brooklyn after handling an "emotionally disturbed person" found weaving in and out of the traffic on Atlantic Avenue.

13

Right In the operations room of the 32nd Precinct in Harlem, Lt.Mike Libretto, ESU City North Supervisor for this morning shift, goes over the tactical plan for a job on 145th Street with ESU and "3-2" officers.

Below The two sergeants who will be supervising aspects of the "hit" on 145th Street - Sgt.John Coughlin, Four-Truck, a recent arrival from the Housing ERU, and Sgt.Juan Garcia, Two-Truck - suit up in Kevlar tactical vests and "Fritz" helmets.

9mm submachine gun or a Ruger Mini-14 5.56mm assault rifle, and two diversionary devices. The cuff men - those who would handcuff the prisoners - grabbed the plastic restraints that are used in mass arrests; the bunker man - the officer carrying the ballistic bullet-proof shield known as the "body bunker" - made sure the flashlight on his Beretta 9mm pistol was in working order. One officer also brought along a dart gun, to knock out any dogs; a crack house's first line of defense can often be a ferocious pitbull. As they geared up and checked their equipment the ESU cops joked among themselves, then finalized the assault plan with Lt.Libretto: hit the lower floors first and work slowly up toward the roof - if the perps wanted to run, it could only be upwards, and plain-clothes would be waiting there.

Once Lt.Libretto signaled to the "3-2" sergeant that his guys were ready, the convoy of precinct and ESU vehicles began its roll to 145th Street. Eight officers squeezed their way into the massive but heavily-laden ESU truck, while the rest rode in their REPs. A van carrying precinct cops went first, followed by the hospital car, an REP, the truck, another REP, and the supervisor's unmarked sedan. The convoy moved slowly up Adam Clayton Powell Boulevard; these days the bad guys are all armed with beepers and cell phones, and the precinct doesn't like to show its hand too early. But at 144th Street everything suddenly kicked into fast tempo - at the radio call *"It's a go!"* sirens wailed and lights blazed, as the blue and white convoy surged forward.

Outside the targeted house, the sight of the vehicles turning onto 145th causes panic. Drug buyers and sellers scatter and run, only to be pounced on by plain-clothes officers who have successfully blended into the graffiti-spattered landscape, and by the "3-2" officers racing out of the van. The ESU vehicles stop short, too, and the officers spill out in a choreographed rush, carrying their weapons, shields, sledgehammers, hydraulic door-opening tools, battering rams, and crowbars through the dilapidated doorway and into the building.

Apartment 3 is the first to be hit. The bunker man places his bullet-proof shield across his forearms, protecting his own head and chest and covering the two men who are using the hydraulic "rabbit tool" to split the locked door apart from its frame. The entry team is supported by two officers aiming their MP5s at the door, and a wary Mini-14 man bringing up the rear. The officers yell "POLICE!" as loud as they can - drug dealers won't usually shoot at the NYPD, especially the heavily armed ESU cops, but they will use their expensive arsenals if they fear they are about to be ripped off by a rival dealer. The rabbit tool does its work in seconds; the officers flood in, and secure the apartment in perfectly synchronized formation. Anyone found inside is immediately placed on the ground and cuffed - not knowing how many "perps" may be encountered, one officer in the formation carries a dozen heavy plastic cuffs tied to his Kevlar vest. Each room is secured in turn by the entire assault crew, with the bunker man charging at point. Apartment 3 is declared secure a few moments later, and two known drug dealers are brought out to the urine-stained hallway to be processed by the precinct officers outside.

Lieutenant Libretto and the ESU officers head straight up the stairs to the next apartment. A plain-clothes officer with a baby face, drug buyer clothes and a holstered Glock looks on from the staircase as Police Officer Vincent Martinez positions his body bunker against the front door of the targeted apartment, and the practised routine is repeated. The rabbit tool does its trick, and again the officers race inside, bellowing "POLICE - GET DOWN!" as they secure the apartment room by room,

Above Expecting the hit to produce quite a few "collars", an officer from Four-Truck readies a handful of the plastic restraint clips that are used instead of regular handcuffs for mass arrests.

closet by closet. (The two female occupants had thought at first that the cops were after back rent, not drugs and guns....) As the ESU cops and plain-clothes officers search the apartment an officer in the alley gets on the precinct band and reports that a box and two guns had been thrown out of a rear window. The precinct cops high-five one another and heave a sigh of satisfaction - drugs and guns are their bread and butter, the fruits of their dangerous work on the streets of Harlem.

In all, nine apartments have been hit in just fifteen minutes - not bad, even by ESU standards. And it is a good hit: a .45 caliber semi-automatic and a .25 "Lady's Special" have been retrieved. No drugs have been recovered; but four suspects have been walked off to a waiting van and a meeting with the desk sergeant for booking. Outside the location, Lt. Libretto debriefs Sgt.Juan Garcia and the team; as the "Loo" discusses the tactical aspects the officers carefully remove their gear and

Left The female "3-2" sergeant listens in as Lt.Libretto (left) goes over the last details of the hit on 145th Street with Two-Truck and Four-Truck officers; the truck is used as a mobile CP.

"Anytime, Anywhere, Any Place": An ESU Overview

Right Showtime - ESU cops race into the building carrying both the most sophisticated and the most primitive door-opening tools, covered by an officer armed with a Ruger Mini-14 rifle.

Below On the stairway a precinct plain-clothes officer (with radio) confirms to Lt.Libretto that there may be four "perps" in the apartment they are about to hit.

Right Officer Vincent Martinez sweats under the weight of his armor and the 13lb. "body bunker", psyched up to lead the team through the door the second that it has been cracked open.

16

Above The choreography of a tactical entry begins - on the left, braced body bunkers and MP5s; on the right, the first man jams the wedge jaws of the "rabbit tool" between door and frame.

Above The second man in line pumps the hydraulic handle of the rabbit tool, cracking the door; a kick finishes the job, and the entry team lunge forward, covered by the bunker man and an MP5. On this job nine apartments were secured in just fifteen minutes.

Right The ESU's part in the process is over; now the precinct officers cuff four suspects for transport to the holding cells at the "3-2". Two guns were recovered on this job.

wipe streams of sweat from their brows. "Good job, guys," proclaims the lieutenant; "it was a good hit." The officers return the MP5s and Mini-14s to their holds aboard the truck, and neatly fold and stow their Kevlar vests, sledgehammers, crowbars and rabbit tool - the gear might be needed in an hour for another tactical job.

*   *   *

"10-13" is the NYPD radio code for "officer needs assistance." There is an old saying in the NYPD: "When a citizen needs help he calls a cop; when a cop needs help, he calls Emergency Service." The men and women of ESU are the elite unit of the New York City Police Department and, in essence, the city's last resort in time of crisis. Some in the department call the ESU officers "super-cops": they are SWAT operators capable of overcoming virtually any tactical situation; they are emergency medical technicians, who can administer life-saving treatment to the victims of any and all disasters; and they are craftsmen, who can rescue trapped survivors from overturned vehicles or from collapsed buildings with remarkable speed and resourcefulness. They are the best of the best that the city has to protect its citizens - and its cops. In the city that never sleeps, where everything and anything can happen, this unit has seen and done it all.

On 6 October 1995 the New York City Police Department will celebrate its 150th anniversary - a remarkable milestone for a department that has been making history ever since the first constables walked their beat around Trinity Church and Park Place, and whose Police Commissioners have included President Teddy Roosevelt. It was the New York City Police Department that wrote the book on urban law enforcement 100 years ago, and it is still putting chapters to bed today.

New York City has been described as many things, and they are all true. The Big Apple is a melting pot of millions and multitudes, a tinderbox of ethnic diversity and aggression, and at the same time the world capital of international finance and entertainment. Today over ten million people call New York City home, and another three million come into the city each day from the outer suburbs.

Geographically, the city is divided into five boroughs. The Bronx is the northernmost borough, bordering Westchester County to the north, separated from Queens by the East River and Long Island Sound, and from Manhattan by the Harlem River. Brooklyn, in the south, was once called the fourth largest city in the United States; it borders Queens to the north and east. The largest borough in size and population, Queens reaches from the skyline of Manhattan along the banks of the East River, to the Atlantic Ocean in the Rockaways, to the border with Nassau County and Long Island in its easternmost reaches. Queens contains both the city's major airports, LaGuardia in the north and John F.Kennedy International in the south; and also Riker's Island, the Department of Corrections facility housing 16,000 prisoners at the entrance to the main runway of LaGuardia in Flushing Bay. Manhattan is, of course, the most glamorous, most famous and most exciting borough. It is home to Wall Street and Broadway, Fifth Avenue and Greenwich Village; it is Chinatown and Central Park, City Hall and Grand Central Station. Yet Manhattan is also the heroin supermarkets of Alphabet City and the Lower East Side, Harlem and Hell's Kitchen, and Washington Heights. Crowded, over-priced and over-developed, Manhattan is a microcosm of the entire city.

In the NYPD atlas the city is divided into borough commands, divisions, and, of course, the venerable precincts. Although the department is run out of "1PP" (One Police Plaza, a red block in lower Manhattan, sometimes referred to as the "Puzzle Palace"), the precincts are the beating hearts of the department, the epicenters of NYPD life. Precincts are as diverse as the city, ranging from a quiet location in Queens such as the "104," covering a large stretch of residential neighborhoods, to the bedlam of Manhattan's Midtown South, honored with the distinction of being the busiest precinct in the world. The precinct is the core of a neighborhood and the symbol of its sense of security.

They are always busy. Walk into any precinct house in the city, at any time, and the activity is mind-boggling. If one happens to stroll into the "3-4" in Washington Heights, Manhattan - one of the city's major narcotics trafficking centers - the desk sergeant will be on the phone, while a passing detective takes into evidence a sawed-off shotgun seized during pursuit of a "perp" somewhere near Riverside Drive. Suspects are brought, in cuffs, before the front desk, and holding cells fill up to capacity before the wagon arrives to carry them off to central booking and arraignment before a judge. Three times a day, at 8.00a.m., 4.00p.m. and midnight, the roll-call is read and a new shift is sent out on patrol.

Some precincts, like the 5th in Chinatown, attract officers from specific ethnic

New York City comprises five boroughs: The Bronx, Queens, Manhattan, New Jersey and Staten Island. Each comes under a Police borough command, sub-divided into divisions and precincts.

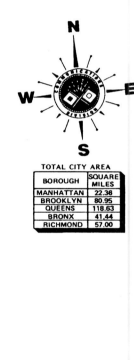

TOTAL CITY AREA

BOROUGH	SQUARE MILES
MANHATTAN	22.36
BROOKLYN	80.95
QUEENS	118.63
BRONX	41.44
RICHMOND	57.00

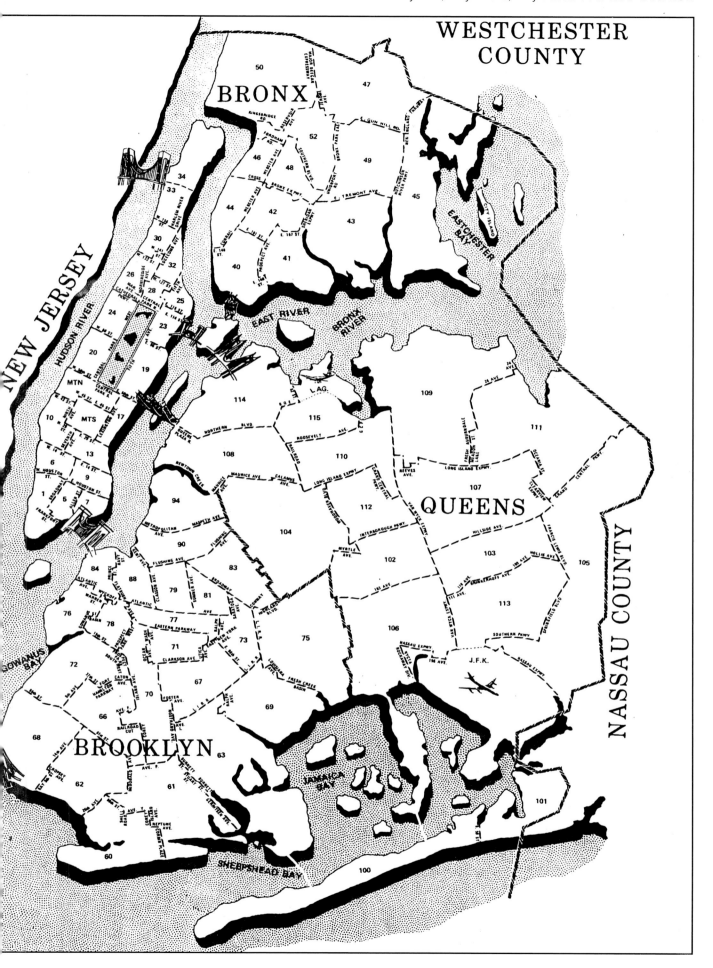

Above The old "fire truck" used by the ESU's forerunners in the 1930s. (Photo courtesy Bob Sobocienski)

groups who speak the native language and understand the local customs. Others, like the "6-7" in Brooklyn's Crown Heights, are so diverse and so flooded with ever-changing cultural groups that a precinct officer would have to be a Spanish-speaking Hasidic Jew born in Kingston, Jamaica, to really fit in.

Most crime experts love to measure a city's level of safety by examining the yearly statistics; they tend to ignore perceptions and measures of deterrence that cannot be pinned down, counted and analyzed. New York City's experts are no different, and most seek to judge how good a job the NYPD is doing solely by the numbers. So, if 1994 can be considered an average year, this is what New York City's crime figures amounted to:

Homicides and manslaughter:	1,274	Down 13.9% from 1993
Arrests for homicides:	*968*	*Up 10% from 1993*
Forcible rape:	2,122	Down 4% from 1993
Arrests for forcible rape:	*949*	*Up 11.9% from 1993*
Robbery:	55,194	Down 12.5% from 1993
Arrests for robbery:	*19,107*	*Up 1% from 1993*
Felonious assault:	29,818	Down 5.2% from 1993
Arrests for felonious assault:	*15,557*	*Up 7.9% from 1993*
Burglary:	68,873	Down 8.4% from 1993
Arrests for burglary:	*6,568*	*Up 4.7% from 1993*
Grand larceny:	56,989	Down 13.2% from 1993
Arrests for grand larceny:	*6,023*	*Up 4.3% from 1993*
Grand larceny auto (GLA):	72,612	Down 13.4% from 1993
Arrests for GLA:	*5,111*	*Up 8% from 1993*

Most officers fresh out of the academy hope to be posted to an "active precinct." A rookie can gather a lifetime's-worth of police experience and skills by working for a few years in a precinct like Harlem's "3-2," the precinct with the most cop killings in the department's history, or the notorious "7-5" in Brooklyn. Working these streets, reacting to crimes of untold brutality and randomness in places where hopes and dreams are no longer the currency of day-to-day life, hones the skills of the officer to the point where he can instinctively pick a "perp" out of a crowd of dozens before knowing what crime has been committed. Many of the rookies who are fortunate enough to be thrown into the fire from Day One on the job eventually end up as detectives and sergeants, with the experience and opportunity to teach a new class of green rookies what life on the streets is all about. Others will serve and protect; and in five years' time will volunteer for the department's elite unit.

The officers on patrol, detectives pursuing their investigations, and supervisors on the beat may have different tasks and stake their claim to different territories; but these brothers and sisters in blue share one reassurance of survival on the streets they safeguard: whenever they need it, they will be backed up by a 350-man unit of E-Men - the NYPD's Emergency Service Unit.

*   *   *

The Emergency Service Unit traces its history to the formation in 1925 of a reserve force of officers who could be called on to perform "extraordinary" rescue assignments; many of these volunteers were also part-time carpenters, welders, riggers and electricians, and the modified fire-trucks they rode were soon to carry a widening range of specialized emergency equipment. Years later, life-saving gear was added to the trucks and the cops were put through emergency medical training. These officers could do any and everything, and prided themselves on being able to rescue any officer or civilian no matter what the situation, from a painter dangling off the Brooklyn Bridge to a clerk trapped in an elevator.

The unit was also among the nation's first mobile tactical response forces, with what was once called the department's Firearms Battalion (as its officers were armed with the old reliable Thompson submachine gun, the unit was also nicknamed the "Machine Gun Squad"); and was the city's first defense against riot situations and large-scale political insurrections. During World War II, it has been rumored, the unit stationed officers atop city bridges armed with elephant guns and binoculars to search for Italian and German midget submarines attempting to enter New York's harbors.

In the years that followed the unit eventually developed into a force called the Mobile Security Unit (MSU), tasked both with responding to emergency situations such as wrecks and disasters, and with addressing dangerous tactical situations that the precinct officers were too lightly armed to contain; its personnel were drawn from the range, and equipped with Suburban vehicles loaded with weapons. In the late 1960s the unit included the legendary Stakeout Unit, a force of NYPD firearms instructors and officers who were concentrated into one effective squad tasked with combating a rash of murders and robberies, mainly at liquor stores; many law enforcement experts agree that the Stakeout Unit was one of the most effective special teams in American police history.

The unit's counter-terrorist tactical role, especially involving hostage rescue, developed in the early 1970s, specifically following the 1972 Munich Olympics massacre. At that time few police forces possessed a special tactics and weapons unit

Left NYPD Chief of Department Louis R.Anemone (center), an innovative and aggressive commander, marches in the 1995 St.Patrick's Day Parade.

that could deal with a hostage crisis; and few forces knew how to deal with the rising tide of criminals armed with heavier firepower than the cops on the beat. Virtually every police force in the world created a special hostage-rescue force following Munich, and virtually every force in the United States created a SWAT unit. New York City already possessed such a resource, but it needed to be expanded.

ESU has always prided itself on the fact that it is the only tactical police unit in the world which is also highly trained and equipped to handle rescue work and emergency medical treatment. In fact, ESU handles just about every type of job imaginable - from EDPs (Emotionally Disturbed Persons) to dangerous animals; from building collapses to plane crashes; from "pin jobs" to SCUBA work. It is its multifaceted character that makes this unit unique in the world - not only in their talents, but in their overall approach to both tactical and emergency rescue work.

ESU officers are the only emergency rescue personnel who may go straight from slicing their way through the mangled debris of a car wreck to extricate an injured motorist, to racing, moments later, to a "hit" against a fortified crack house; who may

Above The NYPD's strong Irish tradition is most obvious on St.Patrick's Day, when many officers take part in the legendary parade up Fifth Avenue in a celebration of everything "blue" and "green".

be tossing "flash-bang" diversionary devices into the apartment of a man wanted on a homicide warrant, immediately before rushing to a Harlem subway station to provide oxygen and medical care to passengers overcome by a pepper mace bomb set off by kids out for kicks. "We treat tactical operations with precision, care and skill," boasts an ESU officer from One-Truck, "and rescue work with the speed and determination of tactical assignments." There is no major emergency in this city, criminal or accidental, that escapes the attention of the ESU, or to which they cannot contribute special skills - from sifting through the rubble of the World Trade Center after it was bombed by terrorists, to providing tactical escort to one of the suspected conspirators of that bombing after he was brought back to the United States to face justice.

If there is one simple phrase to describe the function of the ESU, then it is - according to veteran Lieutenant Bob Sobocienski - "to save lives." The protection of human life is an all-important though sometimes unheralded aspect of the unit's daily work, which the public may never consider unless they themselves are rescued by ESU officers. In many ways these officers are as skilled in providing emergency medical care as the most experienced combat medic, and as comforting and helpful in times of crisis as the most compassionate nurse - qualities coupled, of course, with a properly mordant New York wit.

In any and every scenario, lethal force is the last resort. "We'd rather bore you to death than shoot you," boasts Lt.Sobocienski; "the term 'acceptable casualties' is not in our dictionary. Maybe it's because we are also a rescue unit dedicated to saving lives, but we will do our utmost not to use deadly force." The unit deploys non-lethal weaponry (such as the Taser) which is particularly effective in safely subduing emotionally disturbed persons; robotics are also available for jobs which a machine can handle, avoiding the need to expose an officer to danger. Each ESU officer undergoes advanced training in a variety of specialized skills that can be decisively effective in defusing a potentially lethal confrontation. It should be noted that all unit members are New York State Certified Emergency Medical Technicians (EMTs), and are trained as State Certified Psychological Technicians. There are jobs, however, where civilian and police lives are genuinely at immediate risk, and the ESU has little choice but to mount a tactical response.

*   *   *

Currently, ESU's roster consists of 350 officers (including bosses) - a small number, considering the fact that with 31,000 uniformed personnel the NYPD is the largest municipal police force in the USA and, second only to the Tokyo Police, the largest in the world. Getting into ESU was once considered as hard as hitting the lottery; currently, over 1,500 male and female officers have their names on a waiting list to be even considered for the unit. In order to be considered for a spot in an ESU training class an officer must have at least five years on the job and an exceptional service record. It is extremely helpful if he or she also possesses a useful special skill,

Right Everyday duty on the streets for ESU: Officer James McVey, Two-Truck, discusses the finer points of pitbull extraction with cops from the "2-8" in Harlem.

Left The aftermath of an ESU "barricaded perp" job: a Bronx resident suspected of stabbing a neighbour to death is taken into custody in the confines of the "4-2".

Below A Highway RMP prepares to escort an ESU Two-Truck REP during a divisional assignment in Harlem.

Above "What d'ya' need, boss?" - ESU supervisor Lt.Bob Sobocienski listens while a patrolman reports to Capt.Cassidy, commander of the 25th Precinct, about an ongoing job on Harlem's 116th Street.

such as being an electrician or other craftsman, a diver, or a former serviceman. The skills that many applicants list when volunteering are highly diverse: some worked in construction before entering the academy, some were plumbers or carpenters, others drove heavy rigs. The purpose of the "additional skill" is simple: ESU work involves using heavy machinery and specialized tools, and an ability to improvise. A background in construction is obviously helpful in rescue work involving buildings; and it demonstrates that the officer has a tolerance for heights - he or she might be sent atop a bridge to talk down a "jumper".

The final hurdle before acceptance into ESU is recommendation by a commanding officer - coupled, perhaps, with a nudge from someone in the unit. It always helps to have a sponsor who can recommend and lobby for you, and in a job where absolute personal trust under pressure can be a matter of life or death, word-of-mouth is important - but it won't get you through the psychological and oral exams, or the gruelling interview. The actual Specialized Training School (STS) lasts sixteen weeks; and, apart from the heavy program of tactical instruction, the curriculum covers the following subjects:

Bridge and building rescue techniques (including talking down a jumper, and pulling one in.)
Vehicle and train accident and building collapse extrication (e.g. the collapse on 21 March 21 1995 of a Harlem apartment building, in which three were killed and dozens of injured were trapped under rubble.)
Rigging and line techniques
Welding and burning torch procedures
First aid as first responders
The operation of power rescue tools
Elevator and escalator emergencies and rescues (helpful when a frightened child in a housing project is trapped atop an elevator, thirteen stories high, after "elevator surfing" for kicks.)
Animal control systems (NYC offers a potpourri of "animal jobs," from breaking up the Superbowl of cock-fights in the Bronx to trapping wild raccoons in Brooklyn.)
Water rescue techniques
Helicopter rescue, rappel and medevac
Recognition of bombs and improvised explosive devices
Transportation of bombs and explosive devices
Recognition and rescue relative to hazardous material (HAZMAT)
Operation of specialized vehicles
Dignitary protection and escort
Specialized police apprehension and hostage-rescue tactics
The handing of Emotionally Disturbed Persons (EDPs)
Use of chemical agents
Use of self-contained breathing apparatus
Use of auxiliary electrical generators and lighting equipment
Handling of electrical and gas emergencies
Aircraft emergencies
Forcible entry techniques
Department of Corrections procedures
Crime scene investigations
High-rise structure rescues

Other specialized training includes the three-week Emergency Medical Technician and one-week Emergency Psychological Technician certification courses; a two-week special weapons certification course; a three-day remote tactics (robotics) course; a one-day non-lethal weapons course (the Taser gun, pepper mace and water cannon); and a two-week SCUBA course, known as PADI (Professional Association of Diving Instructors), including basic and advanced certification, dry suit, and search and recovery special certification.

Each phase of the STS must be passed in order to earn a spot on the unit roster, and the intensity of the study is competitive and harsh. Upon completion of the STS requirements each ESU officer is assigned to work with a senior member of the unit, a "rabbi," for a three-month on-the-job probationary period of training and evaluation. Each ESU officer, whether he is fresh out of STS or an experienced E-man in

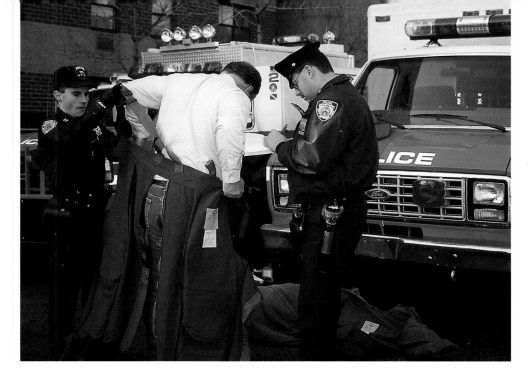

the Bronx with fifteen years on the job, must undergo a variety of refresher and advanced training courses annually. Even though they might do this type of work day-in, day-out on the streets of the city, the refresher courses ensure that they do it right. These courses include:

Three one-day special weapons classes
One five-day specialized training course covering rescue techniques and tactics
One seven-course every three years to maintain EMT certification
Three five-day courses on advanced tactics and techniques
Weekly in-house documentation "trio" training conducted by ESU supervisors
Advanced HAZMAT instruction
Regular drills relative to high-rise fire rescue, ship and aircraft disasters (as well as hijackings), and large-scale Emergency Service Unit responses
One-day non-lethal weapons and tactics refreshers
Six SCUBA dives per year

*   *   *

Getting the chance to wear the ESU baseball cap and dark blue "fatigues" is perhaps the most sought-after distinction in the NYPD. Some hopeful volunteers can wait as long as ten years before they are called in to the Special Operations Division building for an interview. That wait only promises to get longer. New York Mayor Rudolph W. Giuliani (a former federal prosecutor) and Police Commissioner William J. Bratton have engineered the merger of the 31,000-man NYPD with the 2,550-man Housing Authority Police Department (the cops responsible for the city's 324 housing projects), and with the 5,000 Transit Authority Police officers (the cops who safeguard the subways). Since 1994, the 44 officers of the Housing Police's elite Emergency Rescue Unit have been on loan to ESU, serving within ESU Trucks. The Transit Police's Emergency Rescue Unit is also to be incorporated into ESU, swelling its ranks to well over 400 - one of the largest such units anywhere in the world.

The men and women of ESU have enormous tasks and responsibilities in their life out on the streets - duties that can appear, on paper at least, so overwhelming that one would think a force ten times the size would be needed. The "job" on the streets makes the description on paper look clinical and orderly; it is anything but. According to the official NYPD guidelines, ESU's job assignment is as follows:

ROUTINE PATROL FUNCTION (a) Patrol omnipresence; (b) summons issuance and arrests; (c) assist precincts in Community Policing Program efforts; (d) response to priority assignments and crimes in progress.

Above Inside a dilapidated tenement an ESU bunker man awaits further instructions after a "barricaded perp" job in the South Bronx.

WARRANTS (a) Search and arrest, assist in search for evidence and armed perpetrators; (b) apprehend violent felons; (c) assist in tactical planning or raid; (d) provide specialized weapons and heavy vests; (e) assist in search, removal of walls, flooring and structural modifications, especially in narcotics cases; (f) provide entry into premises through battering rams, forced entry tools, secure doors; animal control (pit-bulls, Dobermans, etc.); and (g) provide special equipment, entry tools, Hurst tools, hand tools, lighting.

SEARCHES (a) Crime scene searches, evidence searches (weapons and materials) and collection of same; difficult search areas, elevator shafts, duct work, venting systems, construction sites, sewers, man-holes, street excavation; safeguarding crime scene, perimeter security and police lines; (b) perpetrator searches, provide heavy weapons and vests, secure perimeter, tactics for systematic/safe search, provide specialized equipment and expertise; (c) missing person searches/lost children and adults, special equipment and lighting and difficult search areas; (d) entry areas, access to rooftops and entry holes in floors, walls and other locations.

EMOTIONALLY DISTURBED PERSONS (EDPs) Respond to all EDP runs, mental health removal orders, suicide attempts/jumpers; specialized equipment (Kevlar gloves, EDP bar), non-lethal weaponry (Taser, Nova, water cannon), restraining devices (mesh blanket, Velcro straps); assist EMS in preparation for transport; develop tactical plans for approaching and restraining person with minimal injury to all involved. ESU officers are also trained in bridge and building rescue techniques and suicide prevention dialogue, and trained in robotics, and erecting a net and air bags.

BARRICADED PERPETRATOR/HOSTAGES Establish and secure inner perimeter, develop tactical plans, provide specialized weapons and heavy vests, assist hostage negotiation team; recovery of hostages, apprehension of hostage-takers; provide specialized equipment, bomb blankets, monitoring equipment, surveillance positions, observation teams, special weapons teams and Emergency Rescue Vehicles (ERVs).

CRIME IN PROGRESS RESPONSES Police officer shot, robbery in progress, shots fired, bank alarms/holdups.

OTHER EMERGENCIES Water/ice rescues, disasters, sniper situations, riots/crowd control.

DIGNITARY PROTECTION The Emergency Service Unit is also the department's primary force in providing dignitary protection and VIP security - a monstrous task in a city as large and diverse as New York. This includes covering presidential visits and those by national political leaders, foreign heads of state, religious leaders and other dignitaries requiring special security details and consideration. As New York is a city with a truly international role, headquarters to the United Nations and various international financial institutions, these details are carried out virtually all year round. In performing these duties ESU interacts with state and federal agencies, such as the US Secret Service, the FBI, the New York State Police, and foreign security agencies. ESU supervisors and officers will work together with representatives to develop and formulate escape and rescue routes. In the dignitary protection role ESU utilizes all its vehicles and equipment, including a Counter-Assault Team Vehicle (or "CAT car") to follow motorcades, observation teams and counter-sniper marksmen. ESU also provides additional security assistance in bomb-sweeps and motorcade security - a precarious undertaking on New York's often grid-locked streets and thruways. ESU officers provide additional tactical security to sensitive convoys passing through New York City, such as escorting dangerous felons heading upstate to prison, and large shipments of narcotics being ferried out of the city to be destroyed upstate.

EXPLOSIVE DEVICES/BOMB SCARES The ESU is also responsible for assisting the NYPD Bomb Squad in the event a suspicious package or device is located. ESU units will secure a safe perimeter and follow the "ICE" doctrine (Isolate, Contain and Evacuate.) ESU officers will join in the search for any reported device, and will then

assist the Bomb Squad in its removal in either the bomb truck or a total containment vessel. With the re-emergence of the "Unibomber" - a serial bomber believed to operate out of the West Coast, who was recently behind the murder of a New York City advertising executive in his home in New Jersey - calls of suspicious packages in the five boroughs have increased a hundredfold. At the height of the Unibomber hysteria, when ESU and the Bomb Squad were following one call after another, a subway train in lower Manhattan was fire-bombed. In another odd episode, when Bronx female officers were working undercover posing as prostitutes to arrest "johns," a man driving a van carrying pipe bombs, cans crammed with black powder and a flame-thrower was arrested and his vehicle and home searched by ESU and the Bomb Squad.

* * *

A former mayor of New York City once referred to the Big Apple as a gorgeous mosaic of neighborhoods and ethnic divisions incorporated into one large and glorious city; some, of course, say that New York City is a giant five-borough mental asylum. Whatever one's view, the mosaic analogy is plausible enough - but only because the NYPD, with ESU as back-up, forms the glue that holds the mosaic's intricate pieces firmly in place. Most of ESU's vehicles, quarters, and indigenously produced sweatshirts bear the phrase "Anytime, Anywhere, Any Place!". ESU has "unofficially officially" adopted this motto as its own; and as the following pages will illustrate, it is if anything an understatement.

Above and below An NYPD Aviation Unit Bell-412 kicks up debris as it lifts off an improvised strip in a park in Astoria, Queens. ESU are trained to rappel and fast-rope, and it was from one of these choppers that officers were lowered onto the roof of the bombed World Trade Center on 26 February 1993 to help evacuate victims.

Right and below PO Tom Rowe (who is also the ESU EMT instructor) and PO Doug Bertrand set up with Remington M-24 7.62mm sniper rifles overlooking a southern Brooklyn precinct house during a protective security detail to Mayor Rudy Giuliani. The team scan surrounding rooftops and windows of known drug locations, monitoring any suspicious movement; they are only authorized to use deadly force if they see an individual with a weapon raised.

Left Lt. Sobocienski and Sgt. Martin Garvey act as observers for POs Rowe and Bertrand on a rooftop in Long Island City, Queens, during a job near the 108th Precinct. Sniper work does not entail the non-lethal end of police business; snipers are trained to concentrate for long hours of tedious, patient vigilance - but then, if need be, to terminate their target with a single shot, usually to the head.

Below PO Bertrand, Four-Truck, tracks a possible target through his Leupold Ultra M3 x10 scope. With a father who was a legendary FBI sniper, and a brother serving as a sniper on the San Diego PD's SWAT unit, Doug Bertrand guesses he was probably born to the trade.

2

The Ten Trucks: An ESU Guide through the Five Boroughs

The Emergency Service Unit falls under the command of the NYPD's Special Operations Division (SOD), a command that also controls aviation, harbor, mounted, street crime and highway units. Situated in the old World's Fair Press Building at the northern edge of Flushing Meadows Park in Corona, Queens, near Shea Stadium and the National Tennis Center where the US Open is played each year, the SOD HQ is conveniently located between two of the city's major roadways leading to Manhattan and the Bronx. It is an anonymous location, and many native New Yorkers don't even know that one of the NYPD's most strategic headquarters is in the park that they pass every day while heading for Manhattan or the Bronx on the Grand Central Parkway. SOD is the Mecca of the Emergency Service Unit; 1 Police Plaza might be "the place", but most ESU orders and assignments are handed out through headquarters at SOD.

As a functioning unit on patrol, ESU is divided into ten "Trucks" or squads, spread out across the city's five boroughs. The Emergency Service Squads are attached to regular neighborhood precincts: ESU One-Truck is based in Lower Manhattan; Two-Truck in Upper Manhattan; Three-Truck and Four-Truck in the Bronx; Five-Truck in Staten Island; Six-Truck, Seven-Truck and Eight-Truck in Brooklyn; and Nine-Truck and Ten-Truck in Queens.

Although each Truck has responsibility for its own distinct territory, large scale situations and city-wide emergencies often send them across bridges and borough boundaries for back-up. This could range from a hostage situation in Queens requiring units from the Bronx and Manhattan, to city-wide disasters like the bombing of the World Trade Center on 26 February 1993, when almost every unit in the city was rushed to lower Manhattan to search for victims trapped in the smoke-filled skyscraper.

Each Truck has its own unique personality and field of expertise, even though all ESU officers undergo identical training. Two-Truck in northern Manhattan (encompassing Harlem and Washington Heights), and Eight-Truck in Brooklyn North (in charge of some of the more treacherous stretches of Brooklyn, as well as its nicest neighborhoods) are the busiest in tactical terms; statistics show that they participate in more hits and perp searches than other squads. Six-Truck in Brooklyn South and Ten-Truck in northern Queens are known as the squads that handle the most pin jobs and "53s" (roadway accidents), because their areas of responsibility include long stretches of highways and parkways. All Trucks are extremely busy, however.

Each Truck is also a microcosm of the unique society that is the NYPD, and of the smaller and more selective community that is the ESU. Unlike a precinct house, the Truck "quarters" is the ESU officer's home away from home. All quarters have kitchens, where some of the best meals to be found anywhere in New York City are cooked; all are equipped with cable TV and VCRs; and all are continually buzzing with the noise of three separate police radios monitoring the various precincts which the Truck covers, as well as the ESU/SOD frequency. While the work that they do is extremely serious, a unique *esprit de corps* is evident in each Truck. Each seems to have its resident grouch, its resident cynic, its resident philosopher and monitor of current events, its resident gourmet cook and cultural man-about-town, and, of course, its resident comic.

Next to caffeine and nicotine, laughter is the officers' most accessible defense against stress. If something can be laughed at, it will be, and quarters is no place for the oversensitive soul; only wives and children are off limits. Any chance to laugh is seized upon, whether it be recalling a particular job, or just poking fun at a fellow

Left In the cramped kaleidoscope of New York's streets even an ESU truck on a tactical job can't expect elbow room. Here, outside the 44th Precinct, the crew of Four-Truck's heavy vehicle are quietly preparing for a hit in the University Heights section of the Bronx.

officer. Like most cops, the men of ESU belong to a close-knit family of law-enforcement officers who find it hard to open up to anyone who isn't a fellow officer - their wives and families included. Among themselves, however, they fill any down time with humor. "These guys don't know if they'll be taking a bullet later in the evening, or if they'll see their wife and kids when the shift ends," explains Detective Denis Burke, recalling some not so pleasant nights on the streets of the 75th Precinct. "Laughter soothes their nerves."

If ESU is a microcosm of the department, then the Trucks are microcosms of the sections of the city that they patrol. Every ESU Truck is worth a book of its own; each has its own history and folklore, its somber accounts of death and comical tales of the bizarre. A brief borough-by-borough breakdown may block in their basic characteristics:

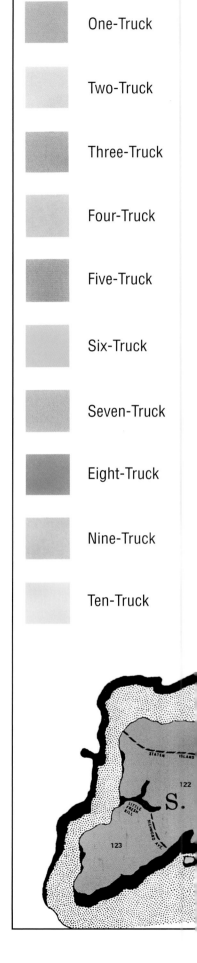

One-Truck

Two-Truck

Three-Truck

Four-Truck

Five-Truck

Six-Truck

Seven-Truck

Eight-Truck

Nine-Truck

Ten-Truck

Manhattan

One-Truck: This squad is known as the "Hollywood Truck", and relishes the reputation and exposure. Situated next to the 13th Precinct on 21st Street in lower Manhattan, One-Truck is based in the most convenient of all ESU locations for media exposure. Beyond its reputation and its steady television and film work, One-Truck is the unit's flagship. Tasked with patrolling the southern half of the island of Manhattan, One-Truck has a zone of responsibility stretching from the very tip of lower Manhattan, the Statue of Liberty and Battery Park, to the river-to-river "border" at 59th Street.

One-Truck is responsible for perhaps the most diverse and cramped part of New York City, including the bustle of Wall Street and the World Trade Center, the congestion and clamor of Chinatown and Little Italy, the trendy streets of Soho and the bizarre haunts of world-renowned Greenwich Village. One-Truck covers midtown with its offices and tourist attractions, and areas like the East Village and the Lower East Side with their narcotics supermarkets, squatter-filled warehouses, and teeming housing projects. Because of its proximity to the Federal Court Houses at Foley Square, One-Truck gets a lot of security work connected with sensitive trials and arraignments. The squad also carry out numerous VIP protection details, safeguarding important guests who may be speaking at the United Nations (inside One-Truck's area of responsibility) or staying at the city's luxurious hotels (most of which are also in One-Truck's half of the island.) Because of the many bridges, high-rise buildings and other landmarks, such as the facade of Grand Central Station on East 42nd Street, One-Truck have also become expert in handling jumpers.

Because the streets of lower and midtown Manhattan are usually too congested for an automobile to reach a speed high enough for any subsequent crash to trap victims, One-Truck doesn't respond to as many pin jobs as the other squads. They make up for it with a generous share of water jobs, involving people unlucky enough to have fallen into the Hudson or East Rivers.

Two-Truck: ESU's busiest unit in terms of tactical work, Two-Truck is the "Jewel of Harlem," responsible for the northern half of Manhattan from the "border" at 59th Street north to the Bronx frontier along the Harlem River Drive and Inwood. Two-Truck encompasses some of the most diverse socio-economic groups in the city - and the world; sometimes a single street separates those who pay $4,000 a month in rent, and those who barely scrape by from day to day on public assistance.

Two-Truck's area of responsibility embraces such neighborhoods as the Upper East Side, the wealthiest enclave in the city, where New York's elite live in spacious brownstones and luxurious condos; the Upper West Side, a mixture of wealthy upper middle class and lower middle class neighborhoods, known for generally liberal attitudes; Spanish Harlem, the Puerto Rican eastern half of the famous neighborhood with Fifth Avenue as the dividing line, where English is rarely heard and the narcotics trade flourishes; Harlem, or more specifically Black Harlem, from Fifth Avenue to the Hudson River, a notoriously high-crime area encompassing some of the busiest precincts in New York (the "2-8" and the "3-2"), where homicide, robbery and rape rates are among the city's highest; and Washington Heights, from Harlem north toward the Bronx, once an enclave for German Jews fleeing Hitler but now almost exclusively Dominican - the city's narcotics capital, it serves as a major conduit for suppliers bringing drugs into the city and (thanks to its interlocking roadways to the Bronx and the George Washington Bridge hooking the city with New Jersey) to all points beyond. Due to its high crime rate it was split into two separate precincts, the "3-3" and the "3-4." Amid these diverse and distinctive areas are parks, housing projects, Columbia University and City College, and two of the city's busiest roadways - the Henry Hudson Parkway along the Hudson River on the city's west side, and the Harlem River Drive and FDR Drive along the east.

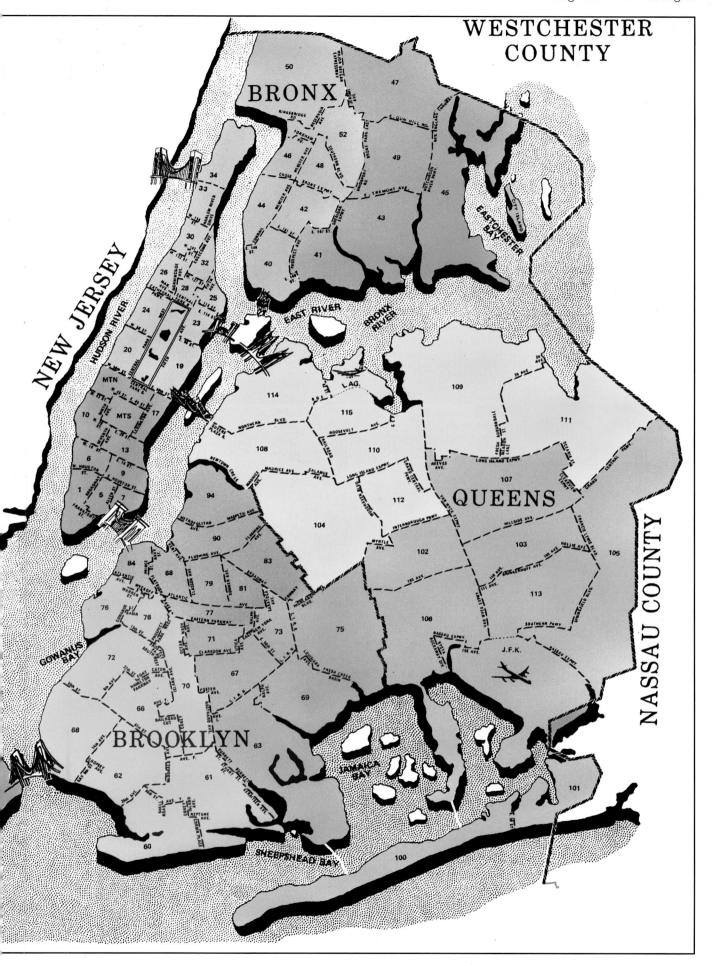

Above ESU's formidable tool on the street - the REP. Here Nine-Truck vehicles illuminate an accident scene on the Van Wyck Expressway, where a tractor-trailer has overturned on the major artery leading to John F.Kennedy International Airport.

Two-Truck officers are among the city's most experienced tactical operators, and participate in more hits and gun runs than any other Truck in the city. Situated next to the 26th Precinct in Harlem, Two-Truck responds to the entire gamut of calls: wild pitbulls and cock-fights, heroin dealers and murders, elevator jobs - and fishermen, plying their trade near a sewage treatment plant, who fall into the Hudson River. Two-Truck also possesses one of the unit's two robot Remote Mobile Investigators (RMIs).

Also known as the "Cotton Club Truck," Two-Truck's quarters are protected by a savage and unyielding canine mascot named Mojo, who will lick any hand bearing food, and curl up against anyone and anything. A Boxer who has been known to drool with the best of them, Mojo greets the officers upon their return from a job, and sulks in a corner when they race out to an emergency.

The Bronx
Three-Truck: Situated behind the 43rd Precinct in the southeastern part of the borough, Three-Truck covers some of the more famous areas of the Bronx, including the 41st Precinct, once known as "Fort Apache." Positioned amid a criss-cross of networking roadways, Three-Truck is a busy rescue outfit called to countless pin jobs on the major arteries such as the Cross-Bronx Expressway and the Henry Hutchinson Parkway. Officers are also summoned to countless EDP jobs due to their proximity to Bronx Psychiatric Hospital, one of the state's five mental health facilities, offering a combination of frayed minds and lax security. With an abun-

Right Snowbound in Harlem, a Two-Truck REP awaits the 4-to-12 shift, and a frigid night's tour of northern Manhattan.

dance of public housing in its domain, Three-Truck gets its share of elevator jobs and tactical work. It is also home to one of ESU's CARV trucks, ready to respond at a moment's notice to a major accident or highway collapse.

Four-Truck: Known in ESU vernacular as "Ice Station Zebra," this is the northern-most Truck in New York City. Situated adjacent to the 50th Precinct in Riverdale, one of the better parts of the Bronx, Four-Truck does not go short of action; it also has responsibility for some of the borough's more desperate stretches such as Marble Hill, University Heights and East Tremont. Because of its proximity to northern Manhattan Four-Truck routinely backs up Two-Truck, especially when the latter's whole strength is committed to a hit, a large-scale pin job, or any type of divisional assignment that leaves Harlem and Washington Heights without proper ESU cover. Four-Truck is also called to handle countless elevator mishaps, as well as various animal jobs. These can range from darting a crack dealer's pitbull, to seizing - on one memorable occasion - 108 roosters and 286 gamblers poised to begin the Superbowl of cockfights. (Had Four-Truck and the ASPCA not intervened, the winner of this prestigious contest was to have received a handsome trophy inscribed *Pelea Mas Rapida* ("The Fastest Fight"), *25 de Marzo 1995, Bronx, New York.*) An air bag vehicle is also based at Four-Truck ready to respond to jumpers in both the Bronx and Manhattan, or further afield.

Above and below The entrance to the "Cotton Club Truck"; and Two-Truck's mascot and venerable dog-about-town, the one, the only Mojo!

Staten Island

Five-Truck: According to one Brooklyn ESU officer who was once pulled over while driving in Staten Island: "The cop came to my window, saw my badge and ID, and said, 'You're a city cop?'" Staten Island is the city's most distant borough, and a strong body of its citizens are actually striving to secede from New York City altogether. The "islanders" regard the rest of the city with some disdain, seeing themselves as a haven of green grass and sanity between Brooklyn and New Jersey. ESU's representation on the island is even known by a different name - Highway Emergency Service (HESE); it is the only ESU squad not under the control of the SOD, but rather of the Borough Command. Five-Truck, as the NYPD still calls it, is busiest with emergency rescue work, highway extrications, and talking jumpers down off the Verrazano-Narrows Bridge; it is also, unsurprisingly, among the city's busiest in terms of water jobs and rescues. Situated behind the 122nd Precinct along the island's main roadway, Five-Truck has become in recent years very busy on tactical assignments, responding to numerous "10-13s" from cops needing assistance, gun jobs, perp searches, and warrants. Because of their proximity to Six-Truck's area of Brooklyn South, Five-Truck units frequently venture into the "Borough of Kings" to assist with back-up.

Brooklyn

Six-Truck: If Brooklyn is a kingdom, then Six-Truck is its regal watch-tower to the south. It is tasked with protecting an area of Brooklyn South from the Brooklyn Bridge and Brooklyn Navy Yards, to the old boardwalk at Coney Island, all the way to Bensonhurst and Canarsie, Red Hook and Flatbush. Based next to the 68th Precinct in Bay Ridge, Six-Truck is a rich stew of everything Brooklyn, and everything New York. According to PO Carl Russo, the Six-Truck safe-cracker and resident comedian: "We cover the best of neighborhoods and the worst, the best people and the worst. We patrol areas where you hear Italian, Russian, Arabic, and even English."

Six-Truck may be summoned to a water job near Park Slope facing the view of the Verrazano and the lower Manhattan skyline; and then respond to a call to the infamous Redhook Projects, a congested area notorious for having the most homicides per square inch in the entire United States. Six-Truck's domain includes highbrow tree-lined residential neighborhoods that - if it weren't for the accents of the locals - one would never recognize as Brooklyn. It also confronts officers with the gun battles and crack sales of Coney Island, where an abandoned Ferris wheel provides a poignant reminder of the borough's more innocent past. Six-Truck also covers Brighton Beach, the now notorious "Little Odessa," where the Russian mafia has set up shop to trade in anything and everything illegal, from hiding gas tax revenue to heroin smuggling.

Seven-Truck: Officers serving in Seven-Truck are a two-borough strategic linchpin. The squad is based near the notorious 75th Precinct in East New York, one of the city's worst; and is responsible for southeastern Brooklyn and the neighborhoods of East New York, Flatlands and Canarsie, Cypress Hill and East Flatbush. From this location they can back up both Six-Truck and Eight-Truck in Brooklyn, as well as Nine-Truck in Queens South.

The patches of (center) the Emergency Service Unit; (left to right, top to bottom) One-Truck, Two-Truck, Four-Truck and Six-Truck.

(Center) The patch of the former Housing Police ERU, now incorporated into the NYPD ESU; and (left to right, top to bottom) those of Seven-Truck, Eight-Truck, Nine-Truck, and Ten-Truck.

Right A slice of life in the Eight-Truck quarters behind the 90th Precinct in Brooklyn North: grabbing a cup of coffee, with half an eye out for the TV news. A photo can't convey the constant crackle and squawk of three radios tuned simultaneously to precinct, division and SOD frequencies (nor the blood-chilling threats from Bud, a dog with attitude, in his rooftop perch).

Eight-Truck: "This Bud's for you!" A visitor to Eight-Truck in Brooklyn North does not need directions or a map to find the squad's quarters; good ears are all that is required, to home in on the ferocious bark of Bud, the Eight-Truck mascot and watchdog, who is known to attempt bodily harm on visiting lieutenants. Eight-Truck is among the busiest in the city, especially in terms of tactical work. Situated behind the 90th Precinct near the elevated Broadway subway line, Eight-Truck is in the middle of some of the worst neighborhoods in Brooklyn; its area of responsibility stretches from the Queens border to the East River where the Williamsburg and Brooklyn Bridges cross into Manhattan. Its officers are involved in more gun runs, perp searches and hits than any other Truck in Brooklyn; in 1993 alone, Eight-Truck participated in over 10,000 gun runs. They patrol such notorious neighborhoods as Bedford-Stuyvesant and Brownsville, where old ladies are routinely beaten up for their social security checks.

Close to freeways, bridges and tunnels, Eight-Truck is the strategic depot for some specialized equipment, including an air bag truck for jumpers in Brooklyn, Queens, Manhattan and Staten Island; the unit's second CARV truck; and the total containment vehicle, for transporting explosives to the range at Rodmen's Neck in the Bronx for safe detonation. Eight-Truck is also quite busy in terms of pin jobs and auto-extrications, as well as various more bizarre calls - this is Brooklyn, after all.

Queens
Nine-Truck: Located behind the 113th Precinct in Jamaica, one of the worst precincts in Queens, Nine-Truck is close to Kennedy Airport and is responsible for the southern half of the borough. Queens is the city's most populous borough and

Right A new day dawns over Brooklyn South, and PO James Helliesen, Six-Truck, heads out to his REP for an 8-to-4 with his partner PO Carl Russo.

one of its most diverse, home to industry, the city's two major airports, and nearly three million residents who speak 100 languages and follow every conceivable religion and way of life known to man. Queens South, as the new NYPD Division is called, stretches from the Nassau County border to the Brooklyn line, from the southern half of the Queens shore along the East River to the Van Wyck Expressway and Hillside Avenue.

Because of the lure of John F.Kennedy International Airport southern Queens has always been criminally active. Convicted mobster John Gotti operated out of the Italian enclave of Ozone Park, hijacking freight from the airport; the drug gangs in Springfield Gardens and St.Albans are just a stone's throw away from narcotics shipments waiting for them in JFK's pick-up areas; and the Rockaways, once a beach resort just a subway ride

Above Sgt.Paul Hargrove, the Ten-Truck sergeant, marches with pride in the St.Patrick's Day Parade up Fifth Avenue.

from the inner city, is now a crime-infested landscape of shacks and projects. These high-crime locations ensure that Nine-Truck is among the busier ESU units in tactical terms. There are countless public housing projects, miles of train tracks throughout the southern end of the borough, and hundreds of miles of roadway - some, such as the notorious Interboro and Van Wyck Expressway, providing officers with regular pin jobs. Nine-Truck also gets plenty of trade in terms of water jobs, with responsibility for the Atlantic Ocean beaches of the Rockaways.

Ten-Truck: Only in New York City can a police emergency headquarters have a "no parking" sign stencilled on its garage doors in Korean, but that's Flushing - home of a million languages. Quartered behind the 109th Precinct on Union Street at the border of Chinatown and Koreatown, and responsible for Queens North, Ten-Truck's personnel are among the most experienced rescue officers in the city. Nearby are three of the city's busiest bridges, and three of its busiest highways (in a neighborhood with, allegedly, the city's worst drivers...); and a five-minute race away are both LaGuardia Airport, and the rescue work provided by Flushing Bay.

Ten-Truck officers have been the first on the scene to pull motorists out of flaming wrecks on the Long Island Expressway; and the first in the water to recover bodies from the flooded wreckage of a USAir fuselage. Ten-Truck officers have talked jumpers down off the 59th Street Bridge, connecting Queens and Manhattan, and have pulled trapped workers out of tunnels and sink-holes. Although Queens North boasts some of the city's most exclusive neighborhoods, semi-suburban bastions like Bayside and Douglaston, Ten-Truck also covers the notorious Queensbridge and Ravenswood Houses - drug-infested public housing high-rises where nightly gunfire is as common as the onset of darkness. Ten-Truck has been involved in some of the most desperate tactical situations in the city's recent history: hostage dramas in apartment buildings, and madmen firing wildly into crowded boulevards.

*   *   *

The "truck" is also the term used for the unit's main work-stations, and the two types of vehicles each squad operates are mini-command and mobile rescue platforms.

Left The Six-Truck "Boy car" REP responds to a job in the "6-6" in Brooklyn South.

Above The Six-Truck "Adam" REP shows off its livery on an unseasonably warm winter's morning, with the southern tip of Manhattan in the distance.

Below A display, at Floyd Bennet Field, of part of the extraordinary range of equipment carried by the Emergency Service Unit REPs - here one of the older vehicles, with room for four in the cab; see the text for a list. The variety of gear carried emphasises the ESU's unique multi-role character. (Photo courtesy Bob Sobocienski)

The smaller ESU vehicle is the **Radio Emergency Patrol (REP)**, a cabin full of emergency gear mounted on a 4x4 pickup. Each ESU Truck (squad) usually maintains three REPs, known as the "Adam," "Boy," and "Charlie" cars. Two are usually on patrol in the Truck's area at any given time, and this roving routine puts them in an excellent position to respond quickly to emergencies. Each REP carries a proportion of the unit's emergency rescue equipment, and protective body armor, though the heaviest firepower carried is the Ithaca 12-gauge shotgun. The equipment carried includes:

General equipment: Two high intensity portable lights, two gas masks, two sound barriers, two goggles, one jumper cables, one Slim Jim, two heavy vests, two construction helmets, two ballistic helmets, two ballistic shields, ballistic blanket, battering ram, two shotguns and ammunition, two batons, two hand-lights, HAZMAT book, rescue harness, Larakus belts with carabiners, webbing, and binoculars.

Non-lethal weaponry/EDP equipment: Tasers and darts, Nova stun device and pole, water cannon, shepherd's crook, Kevlar & stainless steel gloves, chemical mace, pepper gas, EDP bar, mesh restraining blanket, Velcro restraining straps, 15in. chain handcuffs, plastic shield.

Hurst tools: Gas motor jaws, cutters, chains, gas can aviation tips, ram, 26ft. hoses.

Pneumatic tools: Pneumatic saw kit, paratech air guns.

Air bags: Three sizes, air bag bottles, air bag regulators, train kit, assorted chocks, cribbing.

Gas powered chainsaw: Stihl chainsaw with tool kit, spare chain, fuel.

SCUBA gear: Two each Viking dry suits, open-cell thermal underwear, AGA masks with regulators, SCUBA tanks and backpack, sets fins, gloves, knives, compass, weight belts, BCD vests, sets rescue line, underwater lights, 150ft. polyprop lines.

Tools & associated equipment: Bolt cutters large and small, wire cutters, ring cutter, lock buster, sledgehammer, Haligan tool, axe, bowsaw, come-along tool, small Haligan, tool box, hacksaw, pry bar, gas key, crow bar, "J" hook, assorted small tools, lock cylinder tool, two "J" chains, chain with hooks, radiac kit, Kelly tool, lanterns, dosimeters, isolation kit, flares, circle cord, reflective tape, oil.

First aid kit: Resuscitator, two 02 tanks, demand valve, suction, assistant masks, cervical collars, KED extrication, spare O2 bottles, sterile water, OB kit, burn kit,

Stokes basket, scoop stretcher, folding stretcher, backboards long and short, blankets, assorted splints, disposable body bags, canvas body bags, DB-45 deodorizer.

Other equipment: Two Scott packs (self-contained breathing apparatus), two one-hour bottles, "B" suit, rubber gloves, electrical gloves, magnet, elevator and electronic kit, two waders, exposure suit, 50ft. line and life ring, kapock vests, work line ½in., work line assorted, life line, dog noose, animal control kit, "Hot Stick," gas masks, goggles and work gloves, reflective tape, sound barriers, 16ft. extension ladder.

Fire extinguishers: One water, one dry chemical, one CO2.

Vehicle stabilization equipment: Four each 6x6 & 4x4 hardwood chocks, assorted wedges, chocks, shoring and cribbing.

In addition to the three REPs each squad also has one much larger vehicle known simply as **"the truck"**. This hulking $250,000 vehicle ($1,000,000 when fully equipped) is the size of a garbage truck; it is usually despatched to large-scale jobs and as back-up for the REPs. The truck carries an extraordinary inventory of rescue and tactical gear, reflecting the almost limitless variety of tasks which ESU is trained to handle:

Gas powered chainsaws: Stihl chainsaw, with tool kit, spare chain, fuel; K-1200 saw with wood blades, steel blades, masonry blades, tool kit and fuel.

Electric power tools: Reciprocating saw, circular saw, high-torque drill, all with spare blades and bits of all sizes.

Radiac equipment: Two Geiger counters, four dosimeters, 20 film badges.

Electrical & lighting equipment: Four 100ft. electrical reels, four 1000 watt & two 500 watt portable lights, two each 1000 watt & 4000 watt light towers, assorted adapters and plugs, two multiport junction boxes.

Hand tools: 40-piece tool box, bolt cutters large and small, sledgehammers 5lb. and 10lb., Haligan tools large and small, two pikehead axes, two flathead axes, bowsaws small, medium and large, carpenter saws, pry bars 12in., 18in. and 24in., lock buster (duck bill), hydraulic bolt cutters, "rabbit tool," various gas and utility shut-off keys, trench shovels, flat spades, various hydrant wrenches, lock puller, "K" tool kit,

Above Before beginning his 12-to-8 shift in northern Queens, PO Dan Reilly of Ten-Truck checks the compressor for the Hurst tool and cutters in the rear of his REP.

Below With the Williamsburg Bridge in the background, the One-Truck "Boy car" attends to a job on Delancy Street on the Lower East Side.

Above An ESU squad's single large truck, seen here in Eight-Truck markings outside the hangar at Floyd Bennet Field. (Photo courtesy Bob Sobocienski)

Right The truck outside Eight-Truck quarters at the "9-0", with some of the multitude of storage compartments open.

Above Inside the spacious truck, Officer Bill Pieszak of Eight-Truck takes a 5.56mm Ruger Mini-14 from its storage compartment for checking prior to a hit scheduled for later that evening.

Left The Hurst tool - "the jaws of life" - stowed in the ESU truck. At 70lbs. this is an unwieldy contraption, but there is no better means of prying accident victims loose from a mangled vehicle. ESU personnel are specially trained in its use by the manufacturers.

Right and below Three-Truck's CARV truck parked behind quarters at the "4-3" in the Bronx, ready to respond to any major incident; and interior view of Eight-Truck's CARV, showing some of the gear carried.

Below Part of the bewildering array of emergency equipment - costed at around $750,000 - carried by the ESU squad truck on its everyday dashes around the streets of New York City; see the text for a list. Note that this vehicle has its lighting towers erected. (Photo courtesy Bob Sobocienski)

Above A special ESU officer recovery van, used to evacuate wounded officers from the field of fire, is deployed during a mock mobilization. It can be driven from within an interior bulletproof compartment.

Kelly tool, grading hooks, "Hot Stick", assorted spikes and nails, rakes and brooms, 24ft. extension ladder, pike polls, 12ft. closet ladder, portable vise, winch (come-a-long), assorted hand tools.

Truck-mounted equipment: 5-ton winch, air compressor, 24 KW generator, light towers, PA radio system, spot and flood lights.

Cutting torches: One Caldo torch with rods, one oxyacetylene back pack, assorted tips, 10ft. hoses.

First aid equipment: Major trauma kit, back boards, cervical collars, resuscitator, spare 02 bottles, KEDs, blankets, assorted splints, burn kit, Stokes basket, scoop stretcher.

Pneumatic tools: Pneumatic saw kit (Wizard), paratech air gun, pneumatic jacking bags in five sizes, control kit, pneumatic air chisel.

Hydraulic tools: 10-ton Porto-power kit; Hurst tools - Hurst 5000 gas motor, Hurst electric motor, Hurst 150 cutters, Hurst Model 32-B, Hurst Model 26 champ, Hurst Model 16 ram, Hurst Model 30 ram.

Specialized equipment: Metal detector, train kit, two 10-ton jacks, hydraulic bolt cutters, electric jackhammer, line gun, hand lights.

Heavy weapons & ammunition: (Adequate...Exact scale of equipment considered classified by the NYPD.)

Tactical equipment: Six ballistic helmets & vests, one "body bunker" ballistic shield, two ballistic barrier blankets, one forced entry door ram, six MSA gas masks with filters, one Kwik-View mirror, one spotting scope.

Rope: Two 200ft. 1/2in. life lines, one 220ft. 5/8in. life line, 100ft. each 5/8in., 1/2in. & 3/8in. manila work lines, 500ft. 1/4in. polyprop cord, four Morrisey life belts, two rescue harnesses.

HAZMAT kit

Self-contained breathing equipment: Two SCBA Scott packs in case, six each spare 60-minute & 30-minute bottles.

Hydraulic tools: Hurst hydraulic manual pump, post support plate, two chains with clevis hooks, two clevis links, clevis pins, assorted tips, fuel, oil, two spare 16ft. hoses.

Vehicle stabilization equipment: Six each 6x6 & 4x4 hardwood chocks, assorted wedges, chocks, shoring and cribbing.

Fire extinguishing equipment: Two pressurized water extinguishers, dry chemical

Right One of ESU's two Remote Mobile Investigators, multi-capable robot devices which can sometimes be sent into a zone of danger instead of exposing an officer to the risk of gunfire or explosives.

extinguisher, two CO2 extinguishers, two 50ft. rolls 1½in. fire hose with nozzles.

Elevator & electrical equipment

Non-lethal weaponry/EDP equipment: Taser and darts, Nova stun device and pole, water cannon, shepherd's crook, Kevlar & stainless steel gloves, chemical mace, pepper gas, EDP bar, mesh restraining blanket, Velcro restraining straps, 15in. chain handcuffs, plastic shield.

Water rescue equipment: Six kapok vests, two ring buoys with 80ft. rope, two shepherd's crooks, exposure suits, two sets waders, four-man inflatable raft (AVON) with oars, one 4hp outboard engine.

SCUBA gear: Two each Viking dry suits, open-cell thermal underwear, AGA masks with regulators, BCD vests, sets fins, gloves, knives and compasses, sets 150ft. water rescue lines, sets weight belts, four 80cu.ft. SCUBA tanks, four Darrel-Allen underwater lights.

Animal control equipment: Two dog nooses, animal control kit.

Assorted rigging equipment: Block, tackle, etc.

*   *   *

Other vehicles in the ESU fleet include a Bomb Truck; a Total Containment Vessel truck; a truck for the two Remote Mobile Investigators; CARV trucks (Construction Accident Response Vehicles); Jumper Response Vehicles (air bags); a Hazardous Material Decontamination Trailer; Generator Trucks; a Photo Observation Vehicle; a Temporary Headquarters Vehicle; and two snowmobiles. Among the more specialized ESU vehicles are two M75 tracked armored personnel carriers, known as Emergency Rescue Vehicles (ERVs), which are used primarily to evacuate wounded officers or civilians from areas under fire.

Above An ESU Counter-Assault Team vehicle ("CAT car"), photographed during periodic VIP protection training at Camp Smith. This more anonymous type of vehicle is the favoured transport for the A-Team full-time tactical units.

Below One-Truck's truck heads back up 21st Street in Lower Manhattan for the acrobatic turn required to slot it back into its garage at quarters next to the 13th Precinct. After experience of negotiating the congested, driver-unfriendly streets of New York City, ESU cops undoubtedly become some of the world's most skilled heavy rig drivers.

3

ESU On Patrol

"109-Henry on the air? Report of a man with a snake on Northern Boulevard and Union. Man reported to only speak Korean. Copy? Central, this is 9-Henry, PLEASE advise ESU! Over, K!"

For Police Officers Dave Kayen and Winston Smith of Eight-Truck, 30 November 1994 was one of those days. It had been an unusually quiet 4-to-12 on the streets of Brooklyn North. After loading their gear onto the Adam REP in quarters they followed a normal patrol route of streets and boulevards, passing intersections lined with crack dealers, and parents trying to shelter their children from the harms of the "hood" protectively escorting them back from school. The SOD radio was quiet this evening, as was division. There were a few close calls - reports of a baby that stopped breathing (EMS took control and saved the child's life), and of a "10-13 (plain-clothes officer needs assistance after being shot"); but these were anonymous and unverified. As NYC is one of the only cities in the country without an automated 911 system that enables the despatcher to get a reading on where the calls come from, 911 is used by jokers and criminals to drive the department crazy.

There were jobs, of course - there are always jobs - but nothing major: a "gain entry" in the Brownsville Houses to assist an ailing elderly man who had fallen out of bed and couldn't get up, and a female EDP walking with wide and glossy eyes in the center of Atlantic Avenue. A call from division sent them across the border into Queens to the 113th Precinct (pronounced "1-13"), ostensibly to search for a perp; but upon arriving at the crime scene, a burglarized house, all they found was a patrolman on a scooter waiting to have ESU lock up the home so that he could get out of the cold.

On the way back Officers Kayen and Smith drove to the Van Wyck Expressway and then on to the Grand Central, turning west on the Long Island Expressway en route to Manhattan and the BQE (Brooklyn-Queens Expressway) which would take them home to Eight-Truck's patch of Brooklyn North. It was just after 8.00p.m.; traffic was bad, but bearable. When they switched the radio from the Queens Division to the local Brooklyn band all seemed quiet enough - until frantic calls reporting a precinct pursuit of a perp suddenly came squawking over division. Patrol cars and street crime vehicles from the 90th Precinct were chasing several black males in a white Honda, heading into Queens on the BQE, after one of them had fired what was believed to be a Tech-9 9mm submachine gun at a group of officers. From boredom to extreme tension, all at the flick of a radio switch....

It is rare for an officer to find himself in exactly the right place at the right time, but that evening in the Adam-Eight REP Kayen and Smith had the bad guys heading straight for them. One catch: nothing is ever that easy in New York, especially slowing down traffic on a major thoroughfare. Pulling over to the divider separating westbound traffic from those coming home into Queens from Brooklyn and Manhattan, Officer Kayen immediately flashed the emergency lights, sounded the siren, and radioed his position in to division, while PO Smith took the Ithaca 37 12-gauge shotgun from under his seat and hopped out, making a precarious journey along the top of the divider as he signalled to the oncoming drivers. Officer Smith was hoping to slow down the eastbound traffic just enough to cause a bottleneck which would squeeze the perps' vehicle to a stop, allowing the pursuing officers to catch up and make the arrest.

You would think that a police officer with a shotgun ordering motorists to stop

Left Officers from Two-Truck (foreground, PO Vincent Martinez, late of the Housing Police ERU) respond to a twelfth-floor apartment in the Manhattanville Housing Project where a wanted perp has barricaded himself. Body bunkers, MP5s and other tactical gear are brought along on these jobs no matter if the perp is wanted for a drug offense or multiple murder; ESU never take an avoidable risk with human lives.

Above Racing under the Broadway elevated subway tracks, the Eight-Truck "Boy car" responds to the call of a barricaded and armed EDP in the confines of the "7-5".

would have an effect on the flow of traffic; but this is New York, remember? Far from slowing, cars sped up, swerving away at high speed. Dave Kayen, clutching his Glock, was trying to report the ongoing chaos to division, when Winston Smith, his 12-gauge raised in anticipation, saw the white "perpmobile" heading toward him at high speed followed by an ocean of blue and white RMPs flashing their lights. "Stop, dammit!" Smith shouted above the roar of the oncoming traffic as he balanced himself precariously on the roadway divider; "STOP!" Raising his Ithaca to the firing position, he placed the white perp car through his sights and caressed the trigger guard; but he could do no more. The white Honda, with blackened windows, raced by undaunted; all Smith and Kayen could do was watch and curse as a dozen patrol cars flashed past in pursuit.

There is nothing more determined than a frustrated cop, and Kayen and Smith set off to search for the white Honda before heading back to Brooklyn. They played on a hunch that the perps had left the BQE at the Meeker Avenue exit - in an industrial area on the Brooklyn-Queens border - to hide until the heat was off; so they rolled the Adam-Eight REP slowly through the deserted loading yards and garbage-strewn streets, past the hookers looking for the evening's first tricks and the sanitation vehicles cleaning up the day's mess. Sitting inside the REP, his adrenalin pump still ticking over nicely, Officer Smith kept the Ithaca nestled on his lap, just in case. These perps were armed and known to be dangerous, and if turning the next corner happened to confront them with the white Honda the ESU cops weren't about to be caught by surprise.

After a half hour of searching through the industrial heartland of Long Island City, Maspeth and Greenpoint the hunt was called off. Adam-Eight returned to Brooklyn for a quick meal before serving out the final hours of their tour.

*   *   *

Patrolling, with its inevitable combination of boredom and sudden tension, is the essence of ESU's work; their REPs are mobile response points that enable the unit to be on scene within moments of any call for back-up from precinct or division. ESU squads operate on a three-shift turnout: the day shift work the 8-to-4, the evening shift the 4-to-12, and the night shift the 12-to-8. Before each shift the two officers in the Adam, Boy or Charlie cars suit up at quarters, grab a quick cup of coffee, and then check their REP's equipment. They perform a quick inventory to make sure that everything is still inside that should be (even Emergency Service Unit vehicles get broken into on the streets of this city), and in working order. Nothing could be worse than to arrive on the scene of a "53-pin" - a car accident requiring the extrication of a trapped victim - only to discover that the Hurst tool and clippers aren't working. While the REPs rove their territory the truck remains in quarters, usually with the Truck sergeant and the officer designated as the vehicle's chauffeur. They respond to the big jobs, and the day rarely goes by without a big job of one kind or another - anything from a major pin job, to a man walking into a precinct house clutching a hand grenade.

While on patrol the officers roam their sectors just as they would if they were precinct cops. They look out for possible crimes in progress, or citizens requiring assistance; they are even required to issue traffic summonses - ten parking and two moving violations per month are the goals for each officer in the process known as "paying the rent." At a rough estimate, about 90% of ESU's jobs are those seen in progress or called in while out on patrol.

ESU's most valuable contribution to the officers out on the street is their role as tactical back-up. When an officer in trouble calls in a "10-13," nothing is more reassuring that the sight of an REP screeching to a halt. Precinct officers and ESU cops will often respond simultaneously at a crime scene or in pursuit of a perp. As the precinct radios are monitored by the patrolling REPs, the units can position themselves to seize a fleeing perp or back up a lone patrol car which might otherwise be vulnerable.

There is no specific time or place when one unit will get one particular type of job; anything can happen at any time, although there are some patterns of probability. Late at night, especially on a weekend when the bars have closed and the drivers are tanked up, is the witching hour for pin jobs. Early in the month is when most people in poor neighborhoods get their government assistance; there is money to be made robbing people who have just cashed their checks. But cops have been shot at in the early morning hours and late at night, at any time of the month and in any kind of weather. Whatever the scenario, whenever it happens and whatever the job, ESU is the beat cop's back-up.

"In the confines of the 3-3, confirmed 10-30 over division of a liquor store being robbed by two black males, red leather jackets, armed with guns at 174 and Broadway," the despatcher announces over the SOD radio as she types the information into her computer back at 1PP. *"Adam-Two, Central,"* the REP responds; *"we're 98 from the pin job on the Henry Hudson, we'll shoot on over there." "Affirmative, K."* In 1994 alone, ESU assisted and backed up MOS (Members of the Service) an astounding 24,234 times. These jobs covered the entire gamut of possible situations in which cops needed a helping hand; many involved gun runs, barricaded perps and hostage situations.

When a patrol car, detective team or anti-crime squad chases a perp through the city's streets, it is usually a routine matter that the uniformed and plain-clothes officers handle efficiently and well. When the perp barricades himself inside a store or an apartment, perhaps taking hostages in the process, then it becomes an ESU job. Contrary to the Hollywood image of SWAT officers bursting through doors and taking down the bad guys with a flurry of automatic fire, tactical situations tend to be the slowest and most methodical type of police work imaginable. Once the perp is confirmed inside a location with no way out, everyone moves slowly and cautiously; the bad guy won't be going anywhere, and time is on the cops' side. Although they are trained and experienced in using their MP5s and Mini-14s, no one in ESU is eager to pull the trigger. No one is eager to get shot at,

Above and below Metropolitan Avenue, Queens - the holes in the windshield are small and neat, and the bloodstains hardly noticeable; but to a trained eye they tell the story of a car-jacking in the confines of the 102nd Precinct which left the victim on the cold pavement awaiting the arrival of Crime Scene Unit officers and the morgue truck, while ESU conducted a perp search.

Above Officers from the "3-2" respond to the report of a gunman robbing a bodega; ESU arrived as back-up, just in case.

Below During a "gun run" in Harlem, Officer Seth Gahr from Two-Truck - a US Army Reserve MP decorated for service in the Gulf War - prepares to enter a possible hiding place armed with an Ithaca Model 37 shotgun.

either. SWAT may stand officially for Special Weapons and Tactics, but a more accurate definition has it standing for Sit, Wait and Talk.

"Our tactical abilities are by no means a *carte blanche* for blazing guns," insists Lt.Bob Sobocienski. On the contrary, unless the perp starts shooting and killing hostages, a strict departmental apparatus of checks and balances operates to ensure that any use of tactical firepower will be solely a last resort. In a typical barricade situation ESU will assume control of the entire inner perimeter, supported by precinct supervisors and, eventually, officers from the Hostage Negotiations Team (HNT). A sergeant Truck supervisor can assemble his men outside a location in full gear ready to go in at a moment's notice; but only the ESU supervisor, usually one of the three city-wide supervising lieutenants, can actually take the responsibility to send the officers through the door. And the ESU supervisor will give the green light only after the precinct duty captain has authorized the job. If a duty captain, whether through tactical inexperience or obstinacy, insists on ordering the ESU officers to perform a task that the ESU supervisor believes too risky, the supervisor will contact the ESU patrol captain.

"Sometimes," explains Lt.Mike Libretto, "the precinct captain knows little about tactical work, even though he may think he does. There was an occasion when one wanted to throw a ballistic blanket across the window of an apartment where a barricaded perp was holding a hostage at gunpoint. We felt that the blanket would not only shield the perp from our fire, but would inhibit our sniper team's ability to observe what was going on inside the apartment. The duty captain was adamant, however, and I had to take it to my supervisor." There are times when such tactical disagreements are passed all the way up to the level of inspector or even beyond. This is not an overseas war zone, but an American city crammed with innocent bystanders, and command responsibility is taken very seriously. To the ESU nothing is more precious than saving a life - be it an officer's, a civilian's, or even the perp's.

Sometimes, tactical back-up jobs tend to be a bit more involved than helping out the precinct; occasionally they find ESU heading out of the city, or even out of the state. In November 1994 nine ESU cops were sent to Orangetown, in Rockland County in upstate New York, to help local police end a barricaded gun job; two RMI robots were brought up from the city, along with the ESU sniper team, and the 38-hour stand-off was brought to a peaceful conclusion. In March 1995 ESU officers from Two-Truck crossed the George Washington Bridge across the Hudson River into New Jersey to chase four youths in a stolen car who had opened fire on them during a routine traffic stop on West 155th Street. During a wild chase the perps fired at the pursuing ESU and NYPD vehicles right across Route 4 into Teaneck, New Jersey, where they were met by local Jersey cops. The sight of the shotgun-armed ESU officers searching for the perps amid the suburban gentility of New Jersey made a striking contrast (eventually, one of the perps was captured hiding under someone's porch.)

Sometimes ESU has backed up patrol cops under the most bizarre and terrifying circumstances. On Sunday night, 18 December 1994, Wen Ping Hsu, a deranged 46-year-old immigrant from Taiwan, shot and killed his landlord Chang Ming Lee in Elmhurst, Queens. He then proceeded to the Tung Shing House Chinese restaurant on Queens Boulevard, in the confines of the "1-12," where he shot and killed Mr.Lee's wife Shirly Yim as she worked behind the cash register. Fleeing west on Queens Boulevard toward the Long Island Expressway, Hsu was followed by the restaurant manager, David Yuksham; Yuksham was shot in the leg and seriously wounded.

Across the street from the restaurant, an officer from the "1-12" was manning a post outside a strip club called Wiggles (a scene of neighborhood protests) when he witnessed the shooting. Calling in a "10-13 shots fired", and radioing for back-up as he raced across the four-lane boulevard revolver in hand, he followed the suspect into a ground-level parking garage where Hsu was attempting to steal a car. When precinct patrol cars flooded the area Hsu took a hostage, Lakhraj Dalipram, and fired wildly at the approaching cops from behind his human shield. Police fired back and, tragically, Mr.Dalipram was killed. Hsu retreated deep into the darkness of the garage, lying in wait with a Taurus 9mm pistol and a briefcase full of ammunition. As officers from the "1-12" moved in on him PO Thomas Kohler was hit in the leg, nearly dying when a round pierced his femoral artery; and Officer Charles Martin narrowly escaped mortal injury when shot in his bullet-proof vest.

A Ten-Truck REP was the first ESU unit on the scene, and Officers Glenn Klein and Ray Denninger took the shotgun from their mounted rack and ventured into the garage in search of the mad gunman. Several minutes of chaos and terror ensued, in the dark bowels of an urban cavern soon carpeted with spent shell casings and blood. By the time the rest of Ten-Truck arrived on the scene, along with reinforcing squads from Nine-Truck in southern Queens and Eight-Truck in Brooklyn North, Hsu was dead, cut down as he fired wildly from behind a parked car. "Bullets were hitting everything," a shaken Officer Klein told reporters; "it was like being in a tin can. It was an endless gun battle. He just kept shooting." In all, an astounding 300 rounds of ammunition had been exchanged; Hsu had brought ten loaded clips with him, and had been hit nearly 50 times by a combined fusillade of 9mm and 12-gauge fire. "It was like a bad Hong Kong martial arts movie, the kind you see on cable," said a Queens homicide detective surveying the scene the following morning as he searched nearby stores for stray bullets; "it was nuts."

*   *   *

While Hsu's rampage forced the police to handle him as a murderous thug, he also qualified as - in the ESU vernacular - an "EDP". Emotionally Disturbed Persons are, by the very nature of their illness or addiction, the most sensitive types of cases that ESU encounters on a daily basis. While many observers might comment that all New Yorkers qualify, in one way or another, as EDPs, those who are certifiably

Above Sgt.Eugene O'Connor, One-Truck, sizes up an abandoned warehouse in Alphabet City which is about to be reclaimed by Housing. Entering abandoned buildings used by squatters, addicts (and worse) calls for care; they are often booby-trapped underfoot or overhead, and officers risk getting buckets of human waste tipped over them.

Right The scene of a murderous rampage in Queens on 18 December 1994 when the deranged Wen Ping Hsu, carrying a 9mm pistol and a briefcase full of ammunition, shot it out with officers from the "1-12" and ESU's Ten-Truck in a parking garage on Queens Boulevard. That's not an oilstain.

Below After talking down a Spanish-speaking EDP in a Lexington Avenue subway station Det.Henry Medina, Two-Truck, discusses his evaluation of the patient with EMS technicians. All ESU officers are certified Emergency Psychological Technicians.

crazy are the ones who worry ESU cops the most. These are the wacky drug fiends, the psychopaths on angel dust, the citizens who hear Satan talking, and those who think that they are Christ. There are EDPs who want to immerse themselves in blood and bodily wastes, and those whose minds are functioning on frequencies not known on this planet.

"If they are simply nuts," explains an officer from Nine-Truck, "then we aren't interested in them; but when they want to off themselves, or are violent and are a threat to themselves and others, that's when we get involved." Every night or day of every year, an ESU Truck is faced with an EDP. *"Man with a knife ranting and raving on a street corner of 143rd and Broadway"..."A jumper on the Grand Concourse"..."Barricaded EDP holding his family at gunpoint on Avenue U"* - sometimes these situations are calmed by the first sight of a patrol car's flashing light; at other times the ESU truck can't get to the scene fast enough. In 1994 alone, ESU handled an incredible 33,879 EDPs.

Years ago they were simply known as psychos or loonies; but according to departmental policy, ESU must be despatched to the scene of each reported (and later confirmed) EDP call - be it a jumper in the Bronx distraught over his sexual confusion, or a naked man in Brooklyn covered in excrement and brandishing a machete. No matter what the scenario, ESU officers know that handling an EDP demands great care and intelligence; in a city that is always on the edge, the repercussions can be enormous. "Every time we get a call, we have one name in the back of our minds," explains an ESU officer requesting anonymity; "and that name is Eleanor Bumpers."

On 29 October 1984 officers from Three-Truck in the Bronx responded to a Housing Police call for an EDP inside a project; housing cops trying to serve an eviction notice had been confronted by a very large woman, with a long history of mental problems, threatening to kill them. In the past ESU officers used to handle EDPs in heavy vests and carrying shotguns; the shotgun, in those less thoughtful times, used to be known as the litmus test for an EDP. If the individual were faking his spasm of mental illness or going through the "crazy routine" for attention, then the sight of an officer pumping a 12-gauge would usually restore his grip on reality in a hurry; if he was not sobered by the display of an Ithaca, then the cops knew they were dealing with a truly disturbed individual.

Eleanor Bumpers did not need a litmus test. A

66-year-old grandmother weighing some 300lbs., she had a lengthy psychiatric history. When the officers attempted to enter her apartment she proclaimed that she would kill anyone who tried to evict her. As the officers moved slowly into the apartment, she lunged at them with a 10in. kitchen knife. Fearing for his own life and that of his partner, ESU Officer Stephen Sullivan fired his shotgun twice, killing Eleanor Bumpers. The city erupted. Ms.Bumpers was black, and African-American leaders called for instant retribution on the white cops. Some officers felt that Police Commissioner Ben Ward went too far to meet these calls when he publicly second-guessed Officer Sullivan's use of lethal force. Much to the anger of the NYPD, Sullivan was eventually charged with second-degree manslaughter, though charges would later be dropped as witness after witness testified that, in dealing with the knife-wielding woman, Sullivan was justified in defending the lives of himself and his partner.

In the wake of the Bumpers tragedy the department accepted that new regulations and non-lethal means had to be found to handle EDPs; the department also realized that ESU was the only unit that could handle the task. The non-lethal equipment includes a Taser electronic dart gun, a device that propels two barbed darts connected to a twelve-foot wire which transmits an electronic pulse to temporarily immobilize an EDP. ESU can also call on a pole-mounted Nova XR500 stun device; a five-foot-high plexiglass shield; two half-gallon water cannons (shooting water propelled by 100lbs. of air pressure), to distract and disorientate an EDP; Kevlar and stainless steel gloves, to protect the officer from knife attacks; chemical mace and pepper spray; an EDP bar, an indigenously designed restraining bar manufactured by the ESU Training Unit; and the Arwen Model 37, which fires rubber projectiles. ESU also deploys a wide variety of restraining equipment designed to allow the safe transport of EDPs to a medical facility. These include Velcro restraining straps, designed to immobilize while still permitting medical evaluation and treatment; and a unique mesh blanket, for use with persons believed to be suffering from cocaine psychosis.

EDPs are one of the more difficult aspects of ESU's work; and it is hardly surprising that officers sometimes release the tension of handling such situations by competing in the recollection of bizarre encounters. Some EDP jobs evoke nothing but sadness: crazies who have killed, or have had to be killed. Other run-ins are recalled

Above Officers from Two-Truck preparing to handle a barricaded EDP equip themselves with pepper mace and the high-pressure "water cannon". They will also take gasmasks with them: barricaded EDPs have a tendency to greet officers with home-made devices such as bleach bombs.

Left After entering the EDP's apartment and restraining her on a strapped litter so that she cannot harm herself or anyone else, ESU hand her over to the care of an ambulance crew to be taken in for psychiatric evaluation. Dealing with EDPs is probably the ESU's least favorite job: it is distressing, often dangerous, and exposes them to unjustified criticism in no-win situations.

Above Responding to the call of a "jumper" on Hoyt Street in the Greek enclave of Astoria, Ten-Truck officers work on the apartment door while outside City South Supervisor Lt.Richard Greene attempts to talk the disturbed man off his ledge. He was brought in safely.

with hilarity - inevitably, given the ESU's necessary safety valve of "laugh at the world now, because we could be dead tomorrow."

At Three-Truck in the South Bronx, one cold snowy night, the second squad was feasting on a typically sumptuous spread of meatballs and spaghetti when a call came through for an REP to be despatched to Bronx Psychiatric Hospital. Apparently a patient had escaped, and a search was requested by the precinct. Officer Frank Comastro began laughing as Sgt.Charles Girven, an experienced ESU veteran and Three-Truck fixture, turned from his pasta to despatch the Adam car. "Remember that elevator job a while ago in that puzzle palace?" he reminded Officers Al Rosenthal and Tim Van Schultz. "You remember - someone had fallen down a shaft, and we were called in. When we arrived all the loonies were in the lobby playing imaginary instruments - pots and pans, and their heads - in a psychotic orchestra? Didn't a female security guard pass out on that job?" The laughter was contagious; but a few moments later a report of a missing child in the Pelham Parkway section of the Bronx subdued the mood considerably.

The very fact of being New Yorkers, and having had five years on the job before coming onto ESU, has given most officers experience in handling the city's crazier encounters. They are also taught advanced psychological techniques in STS refreshers; all ESU personnel are certified State Psychological Technicians, and the insights taught on the course are employed with a typical New York flair in establishing dialogue and interpersonal relations with EDPs to defuse volatile situations. Sometimes, however, non-lethal force just isn't an option.

One freezing night in the "3-3" Two-Truck was summoned to West 159th by the call of a barricaded EDP. Precinct cops had tried to serve 32-year-old Mitchell Edey with a psychiatric warrant issued by Family Court, to take the subject into custody for a psychiatric evaluation. They were greeted at the front door of the apartment by the subject with a knife and a hammer attached to his hands; he then barricaded himself inside. Officers from Two-Truck arrived on the scene and attempted to persuade Edey out of his room. Subsequently they tried a water cannon, a Taser, and even pepper mace, but without success. He then went back into his room and emerged with a chainsaw. Two of the ESU officers retreated a few steps to gain some maneuvering room, but slipped and fell. As Edey approached them with the howling powersaw he was shot and killed by an ESU officer with a 9mm Glock.

Some EDPs are not only crazy but also heavily armed. In May 1994 two inmates at a state hospital for the criminally insane, serving multiple life sentences for rape and murder, escaped with a smuggled-in firearm. As both convicts were Brooklyn natives, Six-Truck units were despatched on numerous sightings, and responded by sending in officers armed with heavy weapons and ballistic protection. "If an EDP is a true EDP," claims Officer Jim Helliesen of Six-Truck, "then he's a regular EDP; but an *armed* EDP is a gun job, no matter what the official departmental classification." The two convicts were arrested days later by a joint State Police and NYPD effort.

In their confusion and despair many EDPs often climb buildings or bridges, and threaten to jump in a desperate final appeal for help. When the call for a jumper is received over the precinct or division radio, it is ESU that is sent racing to the scene. Expert ropesmen, ESU cops tie in to a building's roof when inching their way closer to someone threatening to jump; if the jumper goes down, the officers are determined not to be taken along. Handling a jumper is always precarious, and no two jobs are the same.

Officer James McVey, Two-Truck, recalls a woman in Spanish Harlem who was standing on a ledge about fifteen storeys above a playground. Officers had roped in and begun the delicate exercise in diplomacy and confidence-building required to talk someone down, when the subject slipped. Officer McVey managed to grab her hand; determined not to let go, no matter what, he held on for dear life until his partners could pull her in. The jumper was saved, and rushed in for psychiatric evaluation.

Other jumpers prefer bridges for ending it all, and some climb to extraordinary heights. On one jumper job in January 1995 officers from Five-Truck in Staten Island responded to a woman threatening to jump off the Verrazano-Narrows Bridge, whose towers soar 700ft. into the sky. The ESU cops roped themselves in, and slowly made their way to the distraught woman. Officer Keith Claire was leading the effort to save her; and when she turned her back on him, looked up at the sky and then down at the water, he knew she was going to jump. He lunged for her, but she wriggled out of her jacket, and plunged 240ft. into the water. Miraculously, she survived to be plucked out of the Narrows by ESU's back-up on this job, divers from the Brooklyn-based Scuba Team 32.

In the course of trying to save the lives of jumpers ESU officers have climbed bridges, and the sculptured facade of Grand Central Station. Hooked and roped in, they have used sign language to talk down deaf jumpers; and have reasoned on school rooftops with ten-year-old kids despondent over poverty and the drug addiction of their parents. In 1994, ESU responded to 2,674 jumper and suicide jobs.

*   *   *

If there are very few ESU officers who volunteer into the unit in order to deal with EDPs, a great many are motivated by the opportunity to perform rescue work and save lives.

Life in New York City has different value in different communities; and in the poorest housing projects the potential for tragedy is great. Bored youngsters living in high-rise buildings enjoy playing a desperate game called "elevator surfing." Climbing out on top of an elevator, the surfer judges his moment to leap across the six-foot gap when an adjacent elevator passes him on the way up or down. If he wins the game, he lands on top of the other elevator. If he loses, he falls to his death, or dangles helplessly. When that happens it is an ESU officer who must climb a dark and dangerous elevator shaft to extricate either a very frightened child, or the corpse

The remains of a Six-Truck REP broadsided by a drunken driver.

Above, right and below After reports of a "53 pin" over the SOD radio, Two-Truck officers respond to an accident on the West Side Highway.

Right Det. Henry Medina instructs a Highway officer to divert traffic from the scene until fluids leaking from the damaged car can be cleaned up.

Left On a snowy night Officers Dan Reilly (foreground) and Billy Johnson, Ten-Truck, attend to the safe dismantling of what was once somebody's prized automobile. At need, these experienced rescue men can cut a victim out of a mangled wreck in a matter of a few moments; getting the patient to medical care without further injury is the only priority.

Above The spreading power of the Hurst tool - "the jaws of life" - demonstrated during a pin job.

Left Officer Johnson on the Hurst tool. A relatively simple device - though at 70lbs. weight, a monster to carry during long jobs - the Hurst tool is probably the single piece of ESU equipment most instrumental in saving lives.

Right Following a "53 with injuries" on Delancy Street Officer Pete Quinn, One-Truck, helps medical technicians remove an "aided" to the ambulance.

Top and bottom right In a snowstorm, ESU officers in Harlem assist a medevac flight bringing in a critically wounded patient from Westchester County for urgent surgery at Colombia-Presbyterian Hospital.

of a very stupid one. Many of the newcomers to ESU from the Housing Police's Emergency Rescue Unit are already highly experienced in elevator jobs; they were a small unit, working in eleven-man shifts to cover a population of 600,000 people - larger than the city of Boston. "When it came to rescue in housing, we were it," boasts Capt.Ralph Pascullo, a decorated ERU officer who is now one of the ESU patrol captains.

Rich people also have their quirks about the relative value of their lives, recalls Officer John D'Allara of Two-Truck, an expert rescue man blessed with another pre-requisite for the job - a wry, very New York sense of humor. One job involved a seri-ously injured businessman trapped in his $40,000 Lexus on the FDR Drive, with the steering wheel pinning his lungs to his back. When the victim saw Officer D'Allara bringing the Hurst tool (the "jaws of life") out of the truck he appeared to lose his mind, yelling "Don't hurt my car, or I'll sue the city!" "Car? What car?" replied D'Allara; "you ain't got no car!" The Hurst tool sheered through the twisted steel skeleton of the Lexus, and the angry motorist was rushed to Bellevue Hospital. It is probably too much to hope that he used his time there to reconsider his priorities.

ESU officers treat pin jobs as if they were embarking on a hit: with speed, deter-mination, and the utmost professionalism. Arriving at the scene they leap from their REPs and trucks, deploying the necessary gear with record speed. Each ESU offi-cer is certified by Hurst Tool Manufacturers in the operation of the "jaws of life" and other cutting and prying attachments which adapt to the specialized gear. The objec-tive in extricating trapped victims is to remove them safely without exacerbating any injuries, and then to provide immediate trauma first-aid to stabilize their condition until they can be transported by ambulance to hospital. Some ESU officers, like the unit's charismatic EMT instructor Tommy Rowe, become full-fledged battlefield medics at the sight of an emergency; they will refer to the injured party as "patient" rather than victim. It should be noted that ESU is probably the only emergency police unit that can boast an MD (Dr.Victor Politi of Eight-Truck) and a registered nurse (PO Mike Hanson of Six-Truck) in its ranks.

Rescue work tends to attract the media spotlight, and many ESU officers have been lauded for their courage in saving lives. There are no glory seekers in the unit, however, and all the officers know that it is a collective effort. Several years ago, after playing an instrumental role in the rescue of a worker who fell into a manhole, PO Tony Mangiaracina of Six-Truck was approached by a TV show wanting to pro-file him for a special episode on the nation's top cops. Officer Mangiaracina refused, unless all the other officers who had assisted him would also be profiled. The show's producers balked at the notion of collective fame, and chose to use a different police department for their segment.

In one respect, of course, ESU officers approach rescue work differently from tac-tical work: there are no "bad guys" in a pin job. Rescue work involves regular citi-zens, guilty of nothing except the bad luck to have been in the wrong place at the wrong time, and in dire need of immediate and life-saving help. "Getting a call to a pin job, a collapsed building, or any other rescue work gets your juices up," says Officer Carl Russo of Six-Truck. "The victim could be any and every citizen of the city - a total stranger, or a member of my own family."

Sometimes it is fellow members of the NYPD family who are involved in accidents while chasing perps at high speed; sometimes even ESU vehicles are involved in smash-ups, and members of the squad who require emergency care. In early November 1994 an REP from Six-Truck in Brooklyn was broadsided and mangled by a drunk driver. This time Police Officers Vincent DeSantis and Anthony Augugliaro - men who have pulled their share of trapped victims from car wrecks - needed urgent help to escape from the twisted REP before the leaking fuel ignited. Incredibly, what they had given to the city was returned to them on the streets of Brooklyn: several passers-by and motorists risked burns and injury to pull the two officers to safety.

One would not think that pin jobs could be a controversial aspect of ESU's work; but in recent years automobile extrications have become a major source of inter-service rivalry between the ESU and the Fire Department. In most states and cities around the country rescue and EMS work is the domain of what is known as Fire Rescue; but not in New York City. Medical emergencies are handled by the Emergency Medical Service (EMS), private ambulances, ESU and the Fire Department. In the 1970s, when the city regularly seemed to be burning to the ground, the Fire Department didn't want rescue work: the fire chiefs argued that ESU had traditionally handled that task, so why should things change? As the old wooden-framed buildings and tenements burned to the ground or were torn down throughout the city, the Fire Department found itself with less and less work. In

Right and below right On a freezing January morning a painter slipped from an eleven-storey building, amazingly surviving the fall to an adjacent fifth-storey roof, though with massive injuries. Two-Truck officers work urgently with EMS technicians to give him first aid, and assist Fire Department personnel in evacuating him from the roof.

budget-tight times, when inactivity could lead to lay-offs, something had to be done. The Fire Department demanded pin jobs and rescue work; a Mexican stand-off ensued, with political implications, and rivalry flourished.

When a "pin" is reported - a car crash with a motorist trapped - there is usually a mad dash by a FDNY Engine to reach the scene and perform the rescue. Sometimes they have attempted to push ESU officers out of the way; sometimes, it is rumored, they have done worse. "If I had a penny for every time a fireman spit on my back when I was working the Hurst tool," claimed one Brooklyn ESU cop who prefers anonymity, "I'd have enough money to retire to Florida."

During 1994, ESU responded to an incredible 13,241 vehicular accidents and 3,450 non-vehicular accidents. Non-vehicular accidents can be anything from gaining entry to a disabled person's apartment so that medical care can be administered, to using rope and a Stokes basket to lower a 700lb. woman down five flights of stairs so that she can be rushed to the hospital.

Sometimes the rescue jobs received by ESU squads on patrol turn out to be massive in scope and extremely challenging. Virtually all ESU personnel are SCUBA-qualified, making the unit the largest underwater rescue and tactical force outside the US Navy. On two occasions during the past decade ESU officers have ventured into the icy waters of Flushing Bay, racing against the clock to pull survivors and victims out of USAir jets when attempted winter take-offs from LaGuardia Airport ended up in the water.

On 26 February 1993, at 12.18p.m., in the largest ESU rescue operation on record, a city-wide call out brought virtually all of the unit's personnel to downtown Manhattan. "At first," recalls Lt.Bob Sobocienski, "the call came out on the radio of a reported explosion at the World Trade Center, unverified and via 911. Then additional calls came out; and then word that it was a bombing. Nobody could ever have imagined that someone would try and blow up the Twin Towers." At the site of the

bombing ESU played a critical role in evacuating thousands of people from the smoke-filled building, and also helped search through the rubble in the underground parking lot of the Vista Hotel - the epicenter of the blast - for trapped victims. In a memorable example of courage and nerve officers led by Sgt.Tim Farrell rappelled from a NYPD chopper onto the roof of the World Trade Center to rescue stranded and injured victims of the bombing.

ESU is one of the world's largest single purchasers of rescue and life-saving gear, and their knowledge and expertise have been used around the globe. When Hurricane Hugo struck the island of Puerto Rico, an ESU team was en route aboard a military transport within hours. As well as searching for victims, the officers helped restore a semblance of normal life for the survivors of nature's wrath, repairing the water supply to many of the battered island's residents. At their training facility inside a hangar at Floyd Bennet Field in Brooklyn, emergency medical, construction and recovery gear is permanently stowed inside a sealed container, awaiting deployment anywhere in the world.

*   *   *

On 19 April 1995, at 10.04a.m., a fair proportion of the ESU workforce were patrolling the streets of the city during a quiet 8-to-4, and the SOD radio traffic was slow. For the crews back at quarters, checking their gear while they listened to the radio and simultaneously kept an eye on New York One news on cable, the first reports that an explosion had ripped through the Alfred P.Murrah Building in Oklahoma City brought an instant flash-back to that fateful noontime two years earlier, and the scenes they had confronted at the World Trade Center. Bombs just didn't happen in the heartland; and all over the five boroughs officers paid close attention to the bulletins every few moments. Watching the TV footage, many of them could guess that they would soon be heading west.

For years, ESU has been under a Federal Emergency Management Agency (FEMA) umbrella called the Urban Search and Rescue Program; this mobilizes ESU officers, firefighters, and EMS medical technicians into on-call rescue forces available for transport anywhere in the United States or the world. It was just after midnight on the morning of 20 April when ESU Capt.Curt Wargo, leader of the New York Task Force (NYTF-1), and Det.Mike Corr, ESU FEMA liaison, received word that NYTF-1 would be activated shortly. Officers assigned were notified, and mobilized to a staging area at Floyd Bennet Field. From there they moved in convoy to John F.Kennedy International Airport in Queens, where a US Air Force C-141 from McGuire AFB, NJ, waited to fly them and their containerized gear to Tinker AFB, Oklahoma City, for what promised to be a desperate and heartrending search and rescue operation.

Above Officer John D'Allara, an experienced ESU rescue man, watches anxiously as the patient is lowered in a Fire Department "cherry picker".

In all, the 56-strong NYTF-1 counted more than 20 ESU officers in its ranks, including Capt.Curt J.Wargo; Lt.John McArdle; Sgt.James Buscemi, Nine-Truck; Sgt.John English, Seven-Truck; Sgt.Timothy Farrell; Sgt.Juan Garcia, Two-Truck; Det.Michael Corr; Det.Henry Medina, Two-Truck; and POs Joseph Amato; Peter Appice, Ten-Truck; Eric Becker; Peter Conlin, Two-Truck; Michael Curtin, Seven-Truck; Robert Gardella and Michael Hanson, Six-Truck; Manuel Hernandez, Three-Truck; Lawrence Johnson and Thomas Langone, Ten-Truck; Donald LaSala, Seven-Truck; Dennis O'Connell, Mark Rippel, Thomas Rowe, Charles Ruppert; and Kenneth Winkler, One-Truck.

Having seen the destruction inside the World Trade Center was no preparation for the carnage they found waiting for them in Oklahoma City. "The scene of the bombing was like nothing we had ever seen, "recalled PO Manny Hernandez, an experi-

Above ESU divers leap from an Aviation Unit chopper into Powell's Cove on the East River to search for a missing boatman. (Photo courtesy NYPD)

enced E-man from the Bronx. "If the bombers wanted to make a statement, they could have set off the device in the middle of the night, destroyed the building, and made their agenda known. But blowing the place up in the morning, with all those people there...That was a crime against humanity!"

The men of NYTF-1 worked twelve-hour shifts inside the tottering, rubble-filled shell of the federal building in a desperate, though highly professional search for survivors; few could feel more strongly than these dedicated rescue men the importance of finding and freeing the injured and trapped. They laboured feverishly through the long nights, pitting their skills and their tools against the mangled steel and ever-shifting slabs of concrete. Tragically, they found no survivors - only corpses.

For many, the most poignant recovery was the body of a US Marine found early on the morning of Monday 24 April. Four members of NYTF-1 were former Marines, including the ESU's PO Manny Hernandez and Sgt.Juan Garcia (along with EMS technician Ray Bonner), and PO Mike Curtin is a First-Sergeant in the USMC Reserves. Recovering the body after a meticulous search, they maintained the stoic tradition of the Corps; the fallen Marine was brought from the rubble in a Stokes basket, draped with an American flag, and turned over to a Marine Corps honor guard. A moment of silence was observed, and a few tears were shed. The small ceremony carried out by this knot of exhausted, dust-caked officers was so moving, and so appreciated by the Marines on the scene, that word of the ESU's retrieval of their comrade's body travelled all the way to the Marine Corps Commandant's office in Washington DC.

NYTF-1 were in Oklahoma City for a week, being relieved on Wednesday 26 April. Most were sent home; three officers - Detective Henry Medina and POs Bob Gardella and Peter Appice - remained to help the FBI in the search for evidence. These officers had so impressed the FBI with their skills during the World Trade Center operation that federal agents specifically requested their assistance in Oklahoma City.

*   *   *

Most rescue calls are less tragically epic in scale; but just as vital for the victims, and often very satisfying for the officers. On 14 July 1994 in Monticello, upstate New York, a two-year-old tot named Joseph Grunwald accidentally got his hand stuck in a meat grinder which his mother had been using to knead cookie dough. His injured hand was sucked up near the blade, and local medics could not release him. Joe, and the meat grinder, were flown by helicopter to Mount Sinai Hospital. In the emergency room the doctor and the child were met by Police Officers Peter Conlin, Kenneth Daly, Robert Hetherington and Michael O'Keefe of Two-Truck, who had with them a piece of equipment called "The Whizzer" - a small air-powered circular saw used in auto body shops for cutting through metal. For a full hour the officers worked on the meat grinder, taking great care not to cut too hard for fear of further damaging the toddler's hand. At last they succeeded in sawing through the metal augers and freeing the boy; although doctors had to amputate one finger, young Joe Grunwald will regain the use of his hand.

Months later Two-Truck would use the Whizzer once again, though under very different circumstances. Sergeant Patrick Murphy and Officers James McVey and Seth Gahr were summoned to the Marion Hotel, a single room occupancy, at 2612 Broadway between 98th and 99th Streets, after the management complained of a man screaming in agony from his room. When the officers entered they found a naked 32-year-old Hispanic with a pair of military-issue handcuffs clamping one of his wrists to his genitalia. As he had tried to remove the cuffs the locking mechanism had broken and the cuffs began to constrict; the harder he tried to get them off, the tighter they became. One of the officers suggested using a pair of bolt cutters, but in the end the Whizzer was applied. It took 20 minutes to extricate the subject from the embrace of his steel friend - the longest 20 minutes of his life.

*   *   *

It is on patrol that the unit sometimes gets to respond to the weird calls, the bizarre jobs involving animals, vegetables, and anything else that the city's crazies can come up with. In Queens, officers from Ten-Truck responded to a possible search for a perp inside a Korean food market in Flushing; the doors were locked, and there was a scuffling sound coming from inside. While the precinct cops stayed outside, peering into the storefront with their hands on their 9mm Smith & Wessons and .38 caliber Police Specials, the ESU officers ventured in - heavy vests, shotguns and all - only to trace the odd noise to crates full of snakes, many of them poisonous, destined for use in the production of Oriental medicines and potions.

Officer Carl Russo of Six-Truck recalls a Brooklyn animal lover who was being constricted by his pet twelve-foot snake. Together with his partner, Russo attempted to noose the beast, restrain it, or - most urgently - simply to remove it from its owner, who was having the life squeezed out of him before their eyes. When all else failed, they took an axe out of their REP and "hacked the SOB in half."

It was also in Brooklyn that Lt.Mike Libretto and the officers from Eight-Truck responded to an urgent request from the Fire Department concerning a loft. The residents, two quirky New Yorkers who thought that a residential neighborhood was a prime location for a reptilian zoo, had decided that it would be nice to have alligators, boa constrictors and other exotic creatures living in their tub, their kitchen, and even sleeping in their beds; local schools used to take day trips to this fourth floor mini-jungle. When the Fire Department happened to stop by to check on a sprinkler system, the "rubbermen" received the surprise of their lives. ESU was called: *"Emergency Adam-Eight,"* came the laconic summons over SOD radio; *"reports of an alligator in the confines of the 9-O Precinct."* The rest was history.

Above Officers from Ten-Truck in Flushing prepare to mount a water rescue of a man reported missing in the waters north of Whitestone Bridge. (Photo courtesy NYPD)

Below Following their rapid response to the crash of USAir 5050 into the icy waters of Flushing Bay, a squad of bone-chilled rescue men pose for a group photo on the muddy shore. (Photo courtesy Bob Sobocienski)

Above Oklahoma City, April 1995: in the dangerous ruins of the Murrah Building, Officers Tom Langone and Mike Hanson, with rigging specialist Mark Rippel, work with Don LaSala and Joe Amato to rig a large chunk of concrete for removal by crane. (Photo courtesy PO Manuel Hernandez, Three-Truck)

Animal jobs are sometimes humorous (such as PO Jose LaPorte wrestling raccoons out of a tree in the Polish enclave of Greenpoint, Brooklyn), sometimes bizarre (coyotes running loose in Van Cortland Park in the Bronx), but sometimes downright terrifying. The pitbull is the pet of choice among the perpetrator element of New York City, and one of the most dangerous enemies of the NYPD. Left to its own devices, with a normal canine upbringing, experts say that the pitbull can be a domesticated pet. Unfortunately for these animals, drug dealers and other criminals train them to be vicious killing machines. With iron-tight jaws capable of twisting off an arm or leg, the pitbull is one of the strongest dogs around; fed a diet of abuse, cocaine and small kittens, it is also one of the most vicious.

On patrol in Spanish Harlem, Det.Henry Medina and PO James McVey drove by a couple with a small child who were laughing delightedly as they watched their unleashed pitbull biting the head off one of the stuffed dummy animals used as a training aid to make the dogs more vicious; clamping its jaws around the doll in a frenzy of rage, the pitbull had already ripped the large toy almost to shreds. Detective Medina, known for his friendly smile and happy personality, lost his mind at the spectacle of this couple training yet another puppy. "Leash the animal now, and go home," he shouted in Spanish; "go home, now!" The dog owners looked up in disbelief: "Why is he yelling at me - what am I doing?" "These people just don't get it," sighed the exasperated detective; "not until the dog kills their kid." Medina and McVey had just completed a pitbull job involving a "puppy" owned by a drug dealer which had bitten a chunk of flesh from a building worker and had to be darted.

*   *   *

Sometimes what appears to be a routine call can unexpectedly lead to an arrest. In Brooklyn, in the Brighton Beach enclave now known as Little Odessa because of the massive influx of Russian immigrants, PO Carl Russo of Six-Truck and his partner responded to the report of a child locked inside his own apartment. Officer Russo, the NYPD's master safe cracker and lock picker, quickly gained access to the apartment, where a child with a high fever had been locked in by his parents while they went out to party at a local Russian organized crime nightspot. After reassuring the kid, Carl Russo noticed quite a few gun magazines lying on the kitchen table. "Hey kid," he asked with a smile, "where does your dad keep his guns?" "Over here," replied the child, innocently pointing at a closet full of revolvers, rifles and Uzis.

At other times an REP can patrol a stretch of one of the city's five boroughs for a whole shift without encountering a single emergency call - not even issuing a summons. In the vehicle ESU cops monitor the precinct, division and SOD radios, surfing around the wavebands in hope of gaining a few moments' start in reaching the scene if a job is called. Sometimes, crimes occur right in front of ESU cops.

On a recent patrol of the drug-rotten Washington Heights section of northwestern Manhattan the City North Supervisor, Lt.Bob Sobocienski, came across precinct officers conducting a traffic stop. "What'd'ya'need?" asked the lieutenant, and the officers briefly explained that the reason for the vehicular stop was a search for a homicide suspect. A Harlem cop with years of experience in anti-crime, Sobocienski had been taught the ropes by one Lewis Manetta, his former partner of eight years in plain-clothes and today, as captain, commander of the 33rd Precinct. Grabbing his flashlight, Lt.Sobocienski searched the suspect car for drugs, guns or anything suspicious. Neither driver nor vehicle yielded anything; but there was police activity across the street. Plain-clothes officers and patrolmen had closed in on a group of youths who were suspiciously hanging around a bakery, and several fitted the description of the hunted suspect. Guided by long years of experience, a sixth sense and a 360-degree field of vision, Lt.Sobocienski headed straight for one youth in particular who triggered his instincts. Before the individual could even consider fleeing he was grabbed by the lieutenant, and eventually cuffed by a detective following closely behind. As the suspect was driven off to the precinct for booking the officers smiled and joked, pleased that their efforts had helped take one more bad guy off the streets. "Thanks for the back-up, Loo," offered a "3-3" Precinct detective. "Anytime, guys."

*   *   *

On patrol one gets to see a wide range of New York life - especially during the midnight tour. On the typical night of 11 February 1995, PO Billy Johnson and PO

Below Officers Kayen and Smith, Eight-Truck, try to gain access to an apartment where an invalid has fallen over in the bathtub and needs help.

Left The humdrum side of an ESU patrol tour: Officers Johnson and Reilly stop a livery cab driver for a moving violation in Jackson Heights, Queens.

Right Spotting a group of youths about to flee from 33rd Precinct detectives, Lt.Sobocienski collared the one who - based on his 26 years of anti-crime experience - "looked guiltiest". He was right; the suspect, wanted for questioning in a homicide case, is handed over to detectives.

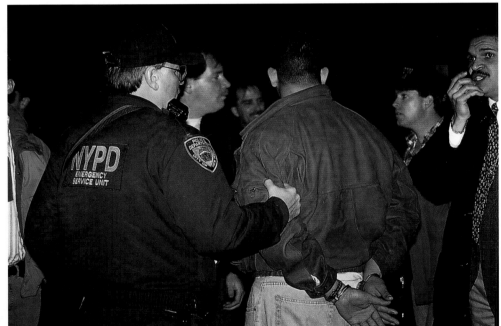

Left An officer from Nine-Truck checks his HAZMAT book with a Highway Patrol supervisor as they respond to an overturned tractor-trailer rig on the Van Wyck Expressway, reported to be carrying hazardous materials.

Right After some of ESU's more challenging animal jobs, a call to restrain an arrested suspect's pitbull on Fifth Avenue and 125th Street is simply routine for PO McVey (left) and Det.Medina of Two-Truck.

Left and below The perp receives a lecture from Detective Medina on the regulations covering ownership of a pitbull in New York City; the puppy, duly noosed and sedated, is tucked comfortably into the back of a precinct RMP by Officer McVey.

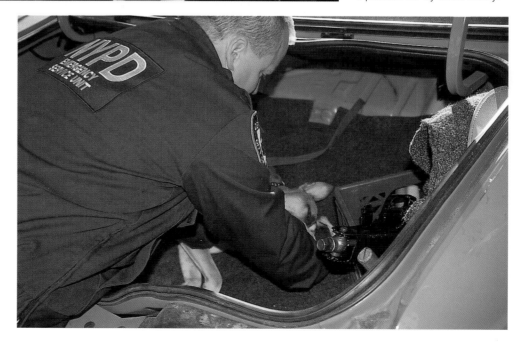

ESU On Patrol

Right Officers Johnson and Reilly, Ten-Truck, take the collapsible ladder from the roof compartment of their REP during a search for fleeing perps on snow-covered rooftops in Astoria.

Danny Reilly of Ten-Truck were the sole ESU presence in northern Queens. Officers Johnson and Reilly are experienced cops, veterans of some nasty precincts, with over 20 years on the job between them. Working in Ten-Truck, one of the city's busiest for pin jobs, they are also expert rescue men (Johnson, it should be noted, is the fire chief of the volunteer outfit in his Long Island home suburb.) The pair work well together, and could probably make a successful stand-up comedy career if they chose. That night it was below zero Fahrenheit, counting the wind-chill, and a dangerously deceptive film of ice had covered the major roads. "A pin job is imminent," guessed Officer Johnson; "wait till the bars close."

On patrol, Johnson and Reilly steadily roved their sector of the borough, from the Long Island border to the Triboro Bridge. They responded to a "door job" in a project. In Jackson Heights they issued a moving violations summons to a livery cab driver named Mohammed who, with the REP behind him, crossed a double yellow line and went through a red light. "Time to pay the rent," Officer Reilly remarked, and the REP raced up behind the cab with lights flashing and siren slicing through the night. As Officer Reilly came up on the passenger side, with a caustic question about local traffic laws wherever Mohammed had learnt to drive, Johnson slipped his hand through the driver's window and removed the keys - just in case.

Below "Relax, it's all over now" - after a two-hour barricade job Officer John Politoski, Two-Truck, reassures a perp taken into custody that he'll be OK.

Motorists in New York City are unimpressed by flashing red lights and sirens. They rarely move out of the way, rarely pull over at first instruction, and tend to view a speeding police vehicle as a convenient pilot for getting through traffic - usually, a speeding REP is followed by a convoy of motorists eager to go through red lights and happy for the fast-moving lane. "New York motorists are incredible," Officer Johnson reflected, as he watched Highway Patrol arrest a drunk driver, and yelled across a warning about the probably explosive danger of lighting a cigarette anywhere near his mouth. "Drivers here give you the finger, don't move, and do everything they can to hinder you," added his partner, "and there isn't anything you can do, because you're racing to a job. Our only consolation comes when we all of a sudden get cancelled, so we find we suddenly have time to pull some idiot over and have some fun."

Back on patrol, Johnson and Reilly continued their tour of Queens North. As they were checking their Hurst tool and metal clippers, just in case a pin job came through, they received a call from the 114th Precinct in Astoria concerning a perp barricaded in an elevator: as ESU covers both barricaded perps and elevator jobs, this was a "double feature." The REP raced along the Grand Central Parkway to 21st Street and the notorious Ravenswood Houses. Entering the projects is always potentially dangerous, and several "1-14" RMPs were waiting for ESU at the entrance to the building where a robber was barricaded inside a stopped elevator. "What'd'you do when you enter a project?" Officer Johnson asked: "You look up - because they always throw stuff down at you."

As Reilly conferred with the anti-crime sergeant as to what this perp had done and whether or not he was armed, an REP from One-Truck arrived with Officers James Derby and Leyland Elliot; they had just performed a 3.00a.m. hit in the Bronx, and had heard of this job over the SOD radio as they rolled back to quarters on the FDR Drive in Manhattan. The stalled elevator's alarm was ringing wildly into the freezing night, but nobody seemed in any hurry - after all, the perp wasn't going anywhere. But as Officer Johnson removed his elevator tool box from the REP the alarm fell silent - the perp was going to try and get off on the first floor. The box was dropped and Glocks were unholstered. Before the elevator doors had fully opened a dozen cops had pounced on the perp. Lying on his stomach, cuffed, and rather obviously under arrest, he chose this moment to feign an unconvincing epileptic seizure, coughing, wheezing and moaning. He then tried an air of injured innocence: "Sergeant, Captain, Inspector Police Officer, Sir.....Why you arresting me?" "Because you're f******g ugly," replied the precinct sergeant, "that's why!"

As the subject was taken into custody, Officers Derby and Elliot crossed the 59th Street Bridge into Manhattan; Johnson and Reilly helped the "1-14" anti-crime squad search for additional perps on the surrounding rooftops, before driving back to quarters along Roosevelt Avenue in the heart of Little Bogota, where the "he/she" prostitutes sell their charms beneath the elevated tracks of the 7-Train. They reached the Truck as the sun emerged on a bright, cold Saturday morning, and filed their paperwork while grabbing a cup of coffee. Before the caffeine could guarantee a few more hours of alertness, a truck carrying hazardous material overturned on the Van Wyck Expressway heading for Kennedy Airport, blocking traffic for nearly five miles back into Manhattan.

For ESU on patrol, it was just business as usual.

Below It's been a long night, and it ain't over yet... Armed with black coffee, Officers Reilly and Johnson resume their patrol in Jackson Heights after successfully defusing a potentially volatile situation - dissuading a drunk from bothering his ex-girlfriend and her family.

4

"Hits" - The World's Busiest Tactical Unit

"It was the best two months of my career as a policeman. All I did was go through doors carrying an MP5 and apprehending perps. Two months of tactical bliss; but then one misses the thrill and rewards of rescue work. The A-Team was nice, but it was like a good bottle of French wine. You enjoy it, savor it, and then once it's done you get on with the rest of the job."

Officer Dave Kayen, Eight-Truck, Brooklyn

Just before noon, 26 October 1994: a typical midday outside the 44th Precinct in the south central Bronx. Two officers were bringing in a suspect who was loudly protesting that "the drugs and money weren't mine, but my bitch's." The elevated subway line on Broadway was serenading the precinct house with the roar and clank of an overhead express heading toward Manhattan as the first ESU squads pulled in, and the clock began ticking. The Police Commissioner Warrant Squad - an *ad hoc* unit made up of picked detectives from the NYPD, Housing and Transit - had scheduled the execution of a warrant on a known cocaine location in the notorious University Heights section of the Bronx. The detectives and the precinct duty captain carried the paperwork, the arrest and search warrants, and the detectives would carry out the arrests and the questioning of suspects. ESU was needed for entry and to neutralize the situation, making the targeted location safe for the precinct and task force to go inside.

Because the "hit" was taking place in the Bronx, Lt.Bob Sobocienski, the City North Supervisor, was to be the ESU supervisor for the job; units from Four-Truck, the squad that usually covers the "4-4," would participate, along with a squad from Three-Truck in the eastern Bronx and Two-Truck from Harlem. The arriving ESU officers parked their REPs and the Four-Truck truck in front of the precinct house, taking care not to block access for the patrol cars. For the Four-Truck officers it had been a routine morning in the Bronx - a couple of gun runs, a perp search and a few EDPs. It had been business as usual, too, for Officers Peter Tetukevich and Seth Gahr from Two-Truck: they had assisted the 32nd Precinct in a gun run for which K9 had been called in; performed life-saving CPR on a 72-year-old man in Riverbank State Park; and had patrolled their sector of Manhattan north of 59th Street.

Inside the "4-4" the ESU officers made their way to the Operations Room, where a captain and a half dozen plain-clothes detectives and anti-crime officers had gathered around a podium to hear the captain's briefing on the location, and what might be encountered there. For officers who had been on literally hundreds of such hits, this was routine. The meeting lasted all of ten minutes, just long enough for a few cans of Coke to be downed, a few cigarettes smoked, and vests and pistols checked.

On arrival at the targeted location the detectives would split into three. One squad would round up any unsavory characters lingering outside a street-level video store, suspected of another line of business; a second squad would race into the alley to check if any evidence was tossed out a rear window or if any perps were fleeing down a fire escape; and the third squad, including the captain, would follow ESU,

Left The A-Team take a sledgehammer to the door of a suspected drugs warehouse in a South Bronx garage, and search it thoroughly and warily. Every time ESU officers enter a location like this they face the risk not only of armed resistance, but also of deadly booby-traps left by dealers to protect their stash from rival gangs.

whose role would be purely tactical - they would gain entry to the apartment above the video store, securing any occupants and evidence until the detectives could go about their work.

The perps were known to carry firepower and were considered heavy duty narcotics sellers; according to intelligence, they cut and cooked the cocaine in the second floor apartment, and sold the finished product - crack - from the video store below. As the ESU officers listened to the TAC plan, some questions were asked: "Is the front door fortified with anything?"; "Are there any booby-traps?"; "Are there any puppies?" A cheerful debate broke out over which borough had the more ferocious pitbulls, Manhattan or the Bronx. Pitbulls are always an intangible during a hit. All officers know that a pitbull can be as serious a problem as a perp (a Four-Truck officer once had a portion of his thigh ripped out, and almost lost something even more precious.) Drug dealers often have their savage "puppies" surgically altered to remove their voice-box, so that the cops can't hear them coming. Some are trained to be so crazy with aggression, and are so doped up, that even a 9mm round won't stop them. (What's more, shooting a pitbull causes the same bureaucratic nightmare as shooting a perp - the discharge of a weapon spawns a mountain of paperwork.)

With all questions answered and all probable scenarios reviewed, the E-men headed outside to their vehicles to suit up; Lt.Sobocienski told them to meet him by the truck in five minutes. It was clouding over, and rain seemed imminent; as the squad opened the storage compartments on their vehicles to get their Kevlar body armor and helmets, several officers glanced at the sky. "S**t," muttered one; "rain and hits are not a good combination. You don't like to be running in full gear on a slippery sidewalk."

Unintentionally but inevitably, suiting up outside the precinct tells the neighborhood that a hit is imminent. Armored and helmeted officers grabbed their Ithaca shotguns from the REPs, and MP5s and Ruger Mini-14s were checked out of the truck. During a hit ESU usually deploy just enough men to secure tactical superiority in a given situation - it is still hoped and prayed that the perps won't resort to bazookas and cannons in their day-to-day dealings on the streets. Each officer took his weapon, checked it, inserted a full magazine, then locked and loaded. Other necessary equipment was also assembled from the truck: a "rabbit tool," sledgehammer, battering rams, a "body bunker" ballistic shield, and diversionary devices or "flash-bangs." Once the rabbit tool or the sledge permits access, tossing in the diversionary device wins the officers a few seconds of deafening, blinding confusion in which to race through the apartment, pounce on the suspects and cuff them. "If you can buy even two seconds on a hit," an officer from Three-Truck pointed out, "then those are two seconds less that a perp has to pull the trigger."

The cops are supposed to arrive for a hit unannounced, proceeding in a convoy that usually consists of a precinct commander's car, a van loaded with officers or detectives, and the ESU vehicles. The hulking truck, though difficult to maneuver, is almost always used, since it is the only vehicle into which six Kevlar-clad officers can fit - four inside the cramped rear compartment, the chauffeur and his partner. Bringing up the rear is usually the supervisor's Crown Vic or Caprice, though he is actually commanding the tactical aspect of the job.

As the detectives emerged from the "4-4" ready for the hit, Lt. Sobocienski gathered his men around him and went over the routine. "Get in quickly and safely, and use the diversionary device once a breech in the door has been made. Let's get it done, guys." "You got it, Loo." Six officers squeezed into the rear of the truck, and the chauffeur gunned the engine. All frequencies were synchronized, and after a final check the convoy rolled.

The drive from the "4-4" to the address in University Heights took ten minutes, at an easy pace and without flashing lights. The bad guys on the streets of the city are a sophisticated lot; armed with beepers and cellphones programmed with speed dialing, look-outs on corner perches can spot an impending hit from a block away and, within seconds, pass the warning for evidence to be flushed away and guns to be tossed out a rear window. Throughout the ride the lieutenant maintained close radio contact with the precinct captain and with the truck's chauffeur. The squalor of University Heights marked these streets unmistakably as a neighborhood rotten with narcotics. Graffiti decorated almost every square inch of brickwork; almost every corner had its bodega (a small, unkempt and overpriced food store), and a wall of the pay phones from where the daily currency of the "hood" is haggled over, sold and eventually delivered.

As the convoy got within a block of the location, all lights were ordered on. The speed rose from 25mph down Morris Avenue to a screeching sixty. By the time the vehicles locked their brakes in front of the targeted location near 183rd Street the

Right and below At a pre-hit Tac meeting at the "4-4" in the Bronx, detectives, plain-clothes anti-crime officers and ESU supervisors review the plan; a Four-Truck officer takes notes on the description of the perps and the weapons they are known to carry.

Above Officers Robert Johnson and Ed Flannery "suit up" beside their REP in front of the 44th Precinct as the neighborhood, accustomed to this sort of activity, goes on about its business.

Right "OK, guys - everybody clear about what they gotta do?" Lt.Sobocienski, City North Supervisor, checks any final questions with an officer fresh from the Housing ERU, armed with a Ruger Mini-14.

Left PO Robert Johnson checks the pin of a diversionary device before tucking it into one of the pouches of his tactical vest and taking his place in the truck.

Below "It's showtime!" The truck slams to a halt outside the targeted location in University Heights, and the ESU team leap out led by the bunker man.

75

Above "POLICE! GET DOWN! KEEP YOUR HANDS UP!" The rabbit tool and sledgehammer do their work, a diversionary device is tossed into the suspect apartment, and in a carefully practised chaos of noise, light and smoke the team race inside.

Right The results of a good hit in the "4-4": drugs, cash, and information.

Above Familiar with the routine, a handful of suspects assume the position outside the video store under the watchful eyes of the Warrant Squad, while Officer Seth Gahr returns a door-forcing tool to the truck.

Right Many of the locals are not too happy that the "drugstore" on their block has been closed down, and ESU cops have learned to watch the rooftops - on occasion they have been the targets of anything from bricks to TV sets, and there have been reports of a perp somewhere out there with a .50 cal.Desert Eagle pistol.

half-dozen individuals in front of the video store were too bewildered to run, or too slow to evade the grasp of the detectives who piled out of their van and immediately ordered buyers and sellers up against the wall. With flashlights and drawn handguns, a second squad of detectives in NYPD windbreakers sprinted into the alley.

Immediately the convoy stopped the back door of the truck swung open and the ESU team made a dash toward the building lobby. The "bunker man" went first, followed by PO Gahr with the rabbit tool, covered by officers carrying MP5s, Ithaca 37s and Mini-14s. Lieutenant Sobocienski followed his officers up a creaking staircase that seemed to threaten collapse under the pounding boots. Pandemonium broke out in the building, the crying of babies mingling with shouts in Spanish echoing through the hallways.

Outside the second-floor apartment the bunker man nestled his shield between his upper torso and head and the doorway; Officer Gahr immediately wedged the teeth of his rabbit tool between the locked door and the frame, and began the short pumping action that spreads the teeth to force the crack open, even if ever so slightly. It did its work to the standard accompaniment of shouted warnings - "THIS IS THE POLICE, STAY DOWN WITH YOUR HANDS UP!" - to enlighten any perp who might imagine that this was a take-over bid by business rivals. As soon as the door showed a wide enough chink a diversionary device was tossed in, detonating seconds later with a deafening crack and a blinding flash. As the room beyond filled up with a dense cloud of smoke the door was kicked in, and the officers piled through with tremendous speed. In a continuous, almost graceful flow of blue and gunmetal the squad swept through the apartment with weapons raised, looking for any sign of movement; visibility was helped by a powerful flashlight and the mini-flashlight attached to the barrel of the MP5.

This time, no cigar: the apartment was unoccupied. Perhaps the perp was downstairs, with his hands already spread out on the brick in front of the video store; perhaps he was at the neighborhood bodega buying malt liquor and potato chips; perhaps he was at his girlfriend's place. But what *was* found in the apartment were large amounts of a white substance on a table, a set of scales, and several thousand dollars in cash. The ESU officers headed downstairs to secure the street while the Warrant Squad went to work. Lieutenant Sobocienski thoughtfully checked the suspect's mailbox downstairs - drug dealers routinely use these as holding safes for the narcotics they intend to sell later in the day - but no luck this time.

Outside on the street the rhythm of an arrest was setting in. The suspects were searched and posed against the wall while the detectives began asking questions, looking to turn chaos into the information needed to slap on cuffs and bring suspects to the "4-4" for processing. The locals, however, weren't too happy. "Yo, yo yo, m****r-f****r, they ain't done s**t," argued a man clutching a 16-oz. can of malt liquor as he stumbled up to the cordoned area. "Take it somewhere else," ordered an officer, "unless you want a trip to central booking." A crowd began to gather, while residents of the building peered out of broken windows reinforced with child-safety

Below After entering a targeted apartment and finding no suspects the A-Team hand over control of the area to detectives who, armed with a search warrant, will sift through it with a fine tooth comb for evidence.

bars. Officer George Hohenberger, knowing from experience what could ensue, kept his eyes moving and a firm grip on his shotgun. In a process likened by ESU officers to "the Indians closing in around the covered wagons," the cops were soon surrounded. Their eyes roved back and forth across the surrounding windows and rooftops. In Washington Heights an officer was killed when a perp tossed a bucket of spackling from a roof. Nobody wants to get hurt, and on these occasions great care is taken to make sure a neighborhood psycho, or a young tough eager to show off, doesn't get the chance to turn a routine job into a trip to the hospital - or worse.

Reinforcements soon arrived from the "4-4", and the locals calmed down and went about their business. ESU's work here was over for this autumn day. The officers chatted briefly with the Warrant Squad detectives before the REPs and truck returned to the "4-4" for a debriefing and

Above Following an A-Team hit in the Bronx, Sgt.Patrick Murphy's crew stow their gear back in the CAT car before heading all the way to Brooklyn, where their services are needed next in the notorious "7-5".

review; Lt.Sobocienski likes to critique each hit, highlighting points that can use improvement. Later the officers from Three-Truck and Four-Truck headed back to their quarters in the Bronx for some paperwork, and the Two-Truck REP returned across the University Heights Bridge into Manhattan. They were hoping to get a sandwich or a Chinese take-out, but knew that the minute they returned to quarters and put the fork in their plate, the SOD radio could summon them to another job.

*   *   *

In 1994, ESU performed a remarkable 1,838 tactical actions, including barricaded-perpetrator and hostage situations. In the first month of 1995 alone ESU has been called to 122 tactical jobs - an astounding number, which makes the unit among the busiest in the world, even more so than the most active comparable European and Israeli units.

Their tactical equipment is also "state-of-the-art" in the field of special unit gear and guns. For years the principal NYPD sidearm was the .38 Police Special revolver, though the department is now up-grading to 9mm semi-automatics - primarily the Glock Model 19. Most ESU officers are armed with these, and Glocks and Beretta 92Ds fitted with flashlights (for use by tactical point men carrying the body bunker) are carried on the truck. The unit's principal 9mm submachine gun is the Heckler & Koch MP5A3 complete with HK94 tactical forearm with built-in light. The

Below The bounty of an outstanding hit - an armory of lethal weapons, from a machete to an Uzi.

unit's primary assault rifle is the American-produced 5.56mm Ruger Mini-14 (an NYPD favorite); and the shotgun carried in REPs, patrol cars and supervisor vehicles is the Ithaca Model 37 12-gauge. The ESU sniper team used to carry the Austrian-produced Steyr Police Sniper weapon, but has recently switched to Remington's M-24 7.62mm system.

Over the past several years ESU's participation in warrant enforcement situations (as "hits" are officially termed) has increased markedly, stretching the unit's manpower to the limits. As a result, ESU created what is known as the "A-Team" or Apprehension Tactical Team. This is a squad of ten officers specifically tasked for full-time tactical duty. They are pulled off their trucks for a period of several months of intensive training and tactical work, and do nothing but hits. The roster is taken from a list of volunteers, until a time comes when all of ESU's 350 (soon to be 400) officers have, at one time or another, served on the A-Team.

Unlike the teams found on most hits, often assembled at short notice from officers of different squads, the A-Team is designed to be a cohesive entity. Each officer is assigned a task, and is expected to learn how his fellow officers operate - be it how long it takes them to bring the rabbit tool to a door, or exactly how they prefer to enter an apartment with Mini-14 in hand. To bond this assembly of officers from the various Trucks the A-Team is sent to the ESU tactical training center at Floyd Bennet Field for a brief refresher course, before being placed on call at the unit's mobile despatch center at a US Army Reserve base in Queens. One of the objectives of the A-Team is for the squad to arrive at the targeted location with a fair degree of surprise, and an unmarked CAT car is deployed for this purpose.

The only jobs they are assigned are hits, or heavy weapons support in major cases such as the shooting of a police officer. There are some days when the A-Team has no work at all, and the various precincts seem almost too quiet. Down time is spent training, working out, reading and cooking. They are always waiting for the phone to ring, for a precinct lieutenant or captain to say, "Be at the precinct in two hours." Sometimes the A-Team finds itself racing from Staten Island to the Bronx, then to Manhattan, and then to Queens. The work is exhausting and dangerous; unlike the routine on the trucks, it does not offer the satisfaction of rescue jobs to break the tension of perp searches and hits. Apart from the constant exercise of cop humor, the only way to relieve the stress is playing *very* close contact games of basketball in split squads, or against the local MP contingent at the base.

At their military-style quarters the team keep a blackboard tally of how they are doing during their two or three months of continuous duty. Toward the end of one A-Team's three-month hitch the score was 46 runs, 43 confirmed hits, 28 guns seized, 79 perps arrested, and two "Oops." "That's the kind way of saying that the precinct screwed up," explained the sergeant leading the team: "it means that we went in

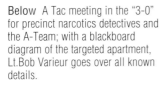

Below A Tac meeting in the "3-0" for precinct narcotics detectives and the A-Team; with a blackboard diagram of the targeted apartment, Lt.Bob Varieur goes over all known details.

only to find it was an innocent location." Most of the locations targeted are very definitely bad, however, and the work sometimes involves joining forces with federal agencies such as the DEA and FBI, executing warrants throughout the city.

Today, most hits are assigned to the A-Team; but under the crime-fighting strategies developed by Mayor Giuliani and Police Commissioner Bratton, precinct commanders no longer have their hands tied when it comes to going after small time drug dealers. Precinct commanders are now like sheriffs in the Old West, given the liberty to make their streets safe through the means and resources at their disposal. Most precinct commanders want bad blocks and bad buildings cleaned up, and most are now ordering increasing numbers of hits. There are days in a particular borough or division (encompassing several precincts) when there are no hits; and there are days when convoys of precinct vans and ESU trucks are seen throughout the city and around the clock. The nature of the individual hits doesn't vary much; a few more recalled examples may capture their essential rhythm - a well-drilled routine climaxing in a burst of effort, sometimes rewarding, sometimes frustrating, but always potentially dangerous.

*   *   *

It is just after 3.00p.m. in the 30th Precinct in Harlem, and the commander's office is empty; so Capt.Barry, second-in-command, takes advantage of the uncharacter-

Above The A-Team launch themselves at the door of an apartment in the "3-0" with rabbit tool and sledgehammer; no matter how often they've done it before, this is the moment of truth, when they will find out whether the location holds any unpleasant surprises not covered in their briefing.

istic peace and quiet to clear up some administrative chores and use the phone. "Have our prisoners been getting their meals from the donut shop around the corner?" the captain asks, annoyed that he has to take care of this personally; but such is the life of a boss. Amid all the apparent chaos of a precinct, between the mountains of paperwork generated by police work and the constant comings and goings of officers, visitors and suspects, a very neat, very New York order is actually maintained. But before the captain can find out where his prisoners are receiving their meals from, his office starts to fill up again with ten visitors, all a few minutes early for the scheduled meeting. They wear ESU uniforms with insignia from different Trucks: they are the A-Team, and there is a warrant to be served.

As the ESU and precinct officers mingle, greeting acquaintances, the two bosses who will be leading the hit begin the TAC briefing. "This is a bad location," announces Lt.Bob Varieur of the "3-0", reading from his clipboard. "We've been here before, so this isn't new to any of us. The location is on the first floor of the building and is known to be used in the distribution of narcotics. We know of two perps, two male blacks, who are in the apartment now. They are believed to be armed." The lieutenant assigns posts to the officers in his command who will secure the exterior of the location once ESU is inside, and Officer Tony Anderson from Nine-Truck asks about pitbulls; none have been reported, but "who knows if they made a trip to the pet store?" The TAC meeting, usually held in the captain's office, is a chance for the ESU cops to see the plain-clothes officers and detectives they'll be working with. In the split-second excitement of a hit, recognizing the good guys is important.

Outside, the A-Team quickly go through the familiar routine of suiting up and checking their weapons. The rabbit tool, a sledgehammer and a battering ram are stowed carefully in the rear cabin of the CAT car, ready to be grabbed in a smooth, well-rehearsed movement. Captain Barry checks that the team are ready; and the vans and squad cars roll.

The ride to the location takes all of three minutes. An anti-crime team is already positioned outside the building, ready to gain entry and secure the hallway the moment they hear the convoy approaching. The "3-0" patrolmen are fast; before their vans screech to a halt the officers have already raced out and flooded the alleyway, detaining four suspicious-looking individuals outside the building who - in the words of the lieutenant - had "perpetrator eyes and felony shoes."

The CAT car pulls to a stop and the officers race out, carrying their gear. It is the usual display of purposeful choreography: officers carrying the body bunker and the rabbit tool are first to line up outside the apartment, followed by two others with MP5s, the supervisor, another MP5, and the Mini-14 bringing up the rear. The rabbit tool forces a gap, and a diversionary device is tossed in. Although they are actually used very sparingly by ESU teams on tactical assignments, this is one of those cases where it would be irresponsibly risky to omit any means of incapacitating reportedly armed perps. The flash-bangs do tend to smoke up an apartment, however, especially one with a rug, and also set off a high-pitched orchestra of smoke detectors throughout the building.

Frustratingly, the perps seem to have been tipped off this time - although nobody's home, a bowl of rice is cooking on the stove and the rear window is wide open. All the rooms are checked anyway, and thoroughly: Lt.Sobocienski orders the officers to look under beds, inside closets and even kitchen cabinets, and to test for false walls - perps can be extremely resourceful when ESU is at the door. Outside, several suspects are on their knees with legs interlocked and wrists cuffed. Whether any of these are the perps the precinct was after with the warrant, the A-Team will never know; that's the work of the detectives, and the team are on a tight schedule. Lieutenant Sobocienski wants to debrief the officers, but time is fleeting. The A-Team has to be in Brooklyn, in the confines of the "7-5", for a hit on a gun location; and Sobocienski himself is running late for a TAC meeting with Two-Truck at the "3-3" in Washington Heights for a hit on a fifth-floor crack store.

*   *   *

There is no particular time for a hit, and they can occur around the clock. Some precinct commanders like the early morning hours best, for obvious reasons. One chilly November morning, Two-Truck has been asked by Deputy Inspector Thomas Sweeney, the 30th Precinct commander, to hit a first-floor Harlem apartment where drugs are reportedly sold. The warrant indicates two Dominicans, both known "shooters" who favour large caliber weapons in any dispute. This is what's known as a "transition hit," mounted in between two shifts, and the extra manpower is welcome. It's still early, but the precinct house is its usual bustle of activity. Deputy Inspector Sweeney is a dynamic officer facing a daunting task. In 1993 the "3-0" was

Below This time, nobody's home; the boss moves into the apartment, watched by Officer Tony Anderson (right), carrying the sledge and a hooked pry-bar.

Left and below Back in the 30th Precinct for a "wake-up call" hit on a pair of reportedly heavily armed Dominican drug dealers early on a brilliant November morning, Sgt.Patrick Murphy, Two-Truck supervisor, runs an eye over his team from the rear door of the squad truck; and Det.Henry Medina checks the "banana" clip of his MP5. Police SWAT units all over the USA (and the world) consider the Heckler & Koch MP5, especially with the integral grip flashlight, to be one of the most efficient weapons available for this type of work.

Above A considerably more primitive piece of equipment, but equally effective in its way: Two-Truck's battering ram.

Right Deputy Inspector Michael Sweeney, 30th Precinct commander, shares a word with Officers Dan Donnelly and Peter Tetukevich before the final slap on the shoulder and "Stay safe"....

Above and left In the cramped hallway outside a Harlem drug den, a 30th Precinct officer covers his ears against the blast of the "flash-bang" diversionary device as Two-Truck officers crowd through the apartment door. Moments later both suspects kneel cuffed under the flashlight of Det.Medina's MP5; the diversionary device threw them off their beds, and before they could reach for any hardware they found themselves underneath a 250lb. officer.

Below As Officer Dan Donnelly looks on, Officer James McVey displays the 9mm semi-auto seized in the suspect's apartment. Few things make ESU cops happier than taking guns off the streets.

plagued by one of the largest corruption scandals in NYPD history, acquiring the tag of "The Dirty Thirty." In the aftermath, Sweeney was determined to take back his precinct - even if that meant block by block.

Although the prospect of a hit is routine for ESU, many police officers not accustomed to tactical work still find the experience unnerving. Consequently, precinct commanders try to share every grain of information about the suspects and the location. At the end of this particular TAC meeting Lt.Sobocienski gives the precinct officers what is by now a routine speech. "Just to let you know, we sometimes use diversionary devices; they make a loud bang - sounds like a huge gunshot. When you hear it, don't think to yourself OH MY GOD and run to the location. We need for you guys to stay at your posts, and make sure the perps don't get away through a rear window or alley."

Outside after the meeting Deputy Inspector Sweeney makes a point of talking for a moment to each ESU officer; his attention is appreciated. The officers share a laugh with the boss, but they are soberly aware that they are going into a location known for both drugs and guns - familiarity does not breed carelessness. As Sweeney and Sobocienski finalize the arrangements the ESU officers grab their weapons and climb into the truck for the three-block ride. Two-Truck supervisor Sgt.Patrick Murphy, a third generation Irish-American cop, clings to the back door holding his Mini-14. His salute as Lt."Sobo" walks by signals that Two-Truck is ready for business.

The ride across Amsterdam Avenue to 149th Street takes them through early morning Harlem traffic, and some expressionless stares. As the convoy comes up to the apartment house Sgt.Murphy opens the truck door and positions himself to leap out. Before Officer Seth Gahr, the truck's chauffeur, hits the brakes, the officers will be out the door. Gahr, an experienced Harlem cop, is also an MP in the Army Reserves, and was decorated during the Gulf War. Driving the truck is a bit more complex than racing around the dunes of Kuwait in search of Iraqis, but he positions the unwieldy beast directly in front of the targeted location. An anti-crime officer holds the door open for the ESU cops as they race inside the building and up to the first-floor apartment. Bunker man PO James McVey reaches the metal door first; he nestles the ballistic shield against it and turns on the flashlight attached to his Glock Model 19. Officer Dan Donnelly and Det.Henry Medina are next in line, followed by Sgt.Murphy, PO Kobel, and Lt.Sobocienski. As Donnelly readies the diversionary device a precinct sergeant clasps his hands over his ears; the expected roar comes just three seconds after the rabbit tool makes its initial breech.

The two perps, fast asleep after a busy night of crack dealing, have no chance to react. Cuffed, they are brought out to the hallway where Det.Medina covers them with his MP5. Precinct officers stand by, shielding the ESU team from other apartment doors that might, just possibly, conceal an armed threat. As the Two-Truck officers return to the sidewalk to remove their gear and stow their weapons, one of the detectives comes out of the building and shows a 9mm handgun to McVey, Donnelly and Medina. "One more gun off the streets...outstanding."

It was a good hit, and a good day in Harlem. As Deputy Inspector Sweeney went to thank the ESU officers for a job well done, an old black woman came up to the precinct commander, placed her hands inside his, and said thank you.

* * *

The officers enjoy the tactical work, but know that it is a never-ending battle: as long as there is the demand, there will always be the supply of narcotics. Even though their tactics are energetic, their small numbers make it an uphill struggle. A few days later the squad was back on another hit, this time at night, and in Harlem's infamous 32nd Precinct. The "3-2" has earned a special place in NYPD legend as the precinct in which the most cops have been killed. This melancholy distinction is evident to any visitor to the station house, where a wall of honor, bearing the photographs of fallen officers, adorns the entrance. Tonight Two-Truck will be joining the 32nd Precinct SNEU (Special Narcotics Enforcement Unit) in a hit on a notorious location where two Jamaicans are running a successful marijuana enterprise. For Manhattan North, it has already been a long day - three hits, with more scheduled.

The meeting at the "3-2" is short and to the point: a diagram of the apartment, a description of the perps, an overall strategy and TAC plan, and a chance to memorize the faces of the SNEU anti-crime officers, who will all be dressed as drug users. The targeted apartment is way up on the sixth floor of a walk-up - not an easy location, considering that the ESU officers are not slender marathoners, but tend rather to be built to subdue and secure.

Right A Tac meeting in the "3-2"; the appearance of the plain-clothes Special Narcotics Enforcement Unit cop in the foreground, with Level III vest and snub-nose .38, underlines the importance of ESU getting a chance to memorize the faces of the other officers they may encounter in the confusion of a hit.

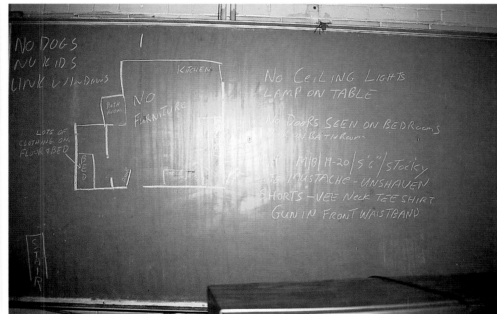

Left The blackboard at the Tac meeting shows the kind of detailed intelligence ESU likes to have before a hit. No briefing is infallible, however, and the E-men can never take anything for granted.

Right The beat goes on....At the "3-3", Lt.James Wallace goes over the Tac plan for a joint A-Team/ Two-Truck hit on a building on 174th Street in Washington Heights where eveery single apartment is considered "wrong".

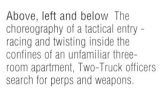

Above, left and below The choreography of a tactical entry - racing and twisting inside the confines of an unfamiliar three-room apartment, Two-Truck officers search for perps and weapons.

The team suit up in the chilly Harlem night, and set convoy formation for the trip to 143rd Street. The Jamaicans are considered likely to be shooters, and the inevitable slight feeling of tension is constructive. Sergeant Owen McCaffrey, Two-Truck supervisor, is a recent addition from Housing and an expert in the tactics of close-quarter confrontations; after all, the projects are notorious drug locations. As PO Seth Gahr checks the flashlight for his Glock 19 and prepares his body bunker, a "3-2" RMP pulls up. It is the H ("Hospital") car, and the driver seems nervous about the responsibility of being the one tasked with transporting any wounded officer to the emergency room.

This location is what is known in the vernacular as a s**t-hole: graffiti decorations, a facade of falling bricks, and smashed windows. The officers, for all their bulk and heavy gear, race up the six flights of stairs with impressive speed and agility. On the top floor they are joined by SNEU cops who have already slunk into the premises and secured the building. As Officer Gahr positions himself to be the point-man inside, the rabbit tool does its magic. So do the diversionary device and Sgt.McCaffrey's sledgehammer. The suspects, in a state of drug-induced mental fog, are cuffed and removed to the hallway, where the SNEU officers take over. "Hey.....Yo man, what's going on, know what I'm saying?," one of perps mutters. "Don't worry, pal, you just won a trip to Disneyworld." As the Two-Truck contingent assemble their gear, Officer Urbina slaps Seth Gahr on the back: "Great job, guys; stay safe!"

*   *   *

It is late one February evening, and the A-Team is back in business - this time in the "3-3." Sergeant Patrick Murphy's A-Team and a squad from Two-Truck will be hitting a known cocaine location in Washington Heights, together with "3-3" Anti-Crime. Operations officer Lt.James Wallace, a dominating and charismatic officer, goes through the TAC plan and the "intel" on the location, a building where all the apartments are considered "wrong." When they finish the hit, they'll have about a half hour to make it to the 42nd Precinct in the South Bronx for another hit on a drug location; and yet another is scheduled for later, in the 115th covering the narcotics-plagued streets of Corona, Queens.

The hits will continue throughout New York City, as will ESU's role as the department's tactical beacon. As a result of the burden of the ever-increasing tactical workload even on the A-Team, ESU has now formed two separate and permanent teams working two shifts a day.

Below This job is done; another is always waiting, somewhere across the city. After a successful drugs hit CNS Lt.Sobocienski briefs a Harlem precinct officer before ESU heads for quarters.

5

"10-13 - Officer Needs Assistance, Officer Down in Brooklyn"

He was all of 26 years old when he was killed. On the night of 15 March 1994 Police Officer Sean McDonald was gunned down in cold blood in the High Bridge section of the Bronx, in the "4-4," as he interrupted an armed robbery at the Filo Fashion Tailor Shop. He was the first NYPD officer killed in the line of duty in 1994. Officer Ray Cannon would be the third.

Friday, 2 December 1994: for the ESU supervisors beginning their 2-to-10 shift on an unseasonably warm winter afternoon it was as average as any day could be. Gearing up back in the lieutenants' locker room at SOD, Lt.Bob Sobocienski, City North Supervisor, and Lt.Richard Greene, City South Supervisor, exchanged smalltalk about the new uniforms - where to place the gold lieutenant bars so that they wouldn't come loose when heavy body armor was worn - and the ups and downs of a departmental boxing match that had far exceeded the promised thrills of its billing. Breaking in a new sergeant, a transfer from the Housing Police's Emergency Rescue Unit, Lt.Greene left Queens for Brooklyn; Lt.Sobocienski headed his Crown Vic supervisor's car north toward Four-Truck in the Bronx. Friday afternoon rush hour traffic was beginning to thicken up on the city's major arteries. The ESU print-out listed a full staff on slate for the 4-to-12 shift. There were no precinct warrants scheduled, and for the first few hours of the supervisor's 2-to-10 shift the radio remained quiet.

At 4.00p.m., Officers Raymond Cannon and Kevin Murphy of the 69th Precinct in Canarsie, Brooklyn, responded to a 911 call of a robbery in progress at Frenchie's Cycle World, in a mini-mall that had been the scene of several robberies in the past few weeks. The two officers, partners since they graduated from the academy in 1990, made their way quickly to the location on Flatlands Avenue and 107th Street, and cautiously entered. Inside, they encountered three black youths walking about, and an older black man who was standing behind the counter. "We got word of a robbery here," Officer Cannon told the youths, his hand resting on his holstered pistol. "No, man, we work here." Both officers, trying to figure out what was going on, let their guard down for a second - but that was all it took. The older man drew a 9mm pistol from his over-sized snorkel jacket, and fired two shots at Officer Cannon; one round hit him in the cheek and the other between the eyes. Officer Murphy returned fire, and a point-blank fusillade erupted; he emptied his Glock's fifteen-round magazine, and reloaded under fire.

Gunfire has become tragically familiar in Brooklyn, and the unmistakable sound brought Sgt.Michael Cafarella and PO James Hunt, two Housing cops on patrol in the Breukelen Projects across the street, racing to the scene. Officer Thomas Taormina, a Highway Patrolman also responding to the "10-13", ventured toward the store, and took a 9mm round in his bulletproof vest. Under fire and with commendable courage, Cafarella and Hunt pulled Officer Cannon out of the store, and he was rushed immediately to Brookdale Hospital. Officer Murphy shot and killed one of the

Above 2 December 1994, 4.57p.m.: an officer from the Transit Police Emergency Rescue Unit, now part of ESU, moves in on Frenchie's Cycle World in Canarsie, Brooklyn, after responding to the shooting of PO Ray Cannon in the 69th Precinct.

Left REPs from all over the city converge on Flatlands Avenue and 107th Street in hope of assisting in the capture of Officer Cannon's killers.

Above City South Supervisor Lt.Richard Greene (center) and City North Supervisor Lt.Bob Sobocienski (right) confer with a dog handler from K9; on this occasion the dogs failed to locate the perps hiding in the basement.

Above right Officers from Ten-Truck in northern Queens ready their RMI robot for action after responding to the call of an officer down and barricaded perps in Canarsie.

perps, later identified as the 30-year-old uncle of two of the other robbers. The other three, one shot in the buttocks, retreated to a storage basement underneath the complex. The shopping mall was cordoned off, additional sector cars were summoned, and a call for help was raised over the SOD radio. Canarsie was Seven-Truck territory.

At 4.03p.m. Lt.Greene and Sgt.Durkin were en route to Six-Truck in Brooklyn in their black Crown Vic, talking about ESU policy and administrative chores, and Lt.Sobocienski had just pulled into Four-Truck in the Bronx, when the first calls came through on the SOD radio: *"10-13, 10-13, confirmed over division. Officer down in the 6-9."* All police cars throughout the city fell silent. *"Officer down, 10-13, reports of officer shot in the face. Suspects held underneath a store at Flatlands and 107th."*

Police officers have an uncanny ability to distinguish between routine radio traffic and calls that hit close to home, and "officer down" is the one that strikes deepest. Radios were turned louder and smalltalk was silenced. Lieutenant Greene and Sgt.Durkin raced from southwest Brooklyn toward the Queens border, while Lt.Sobocienski began a 20-mile dash from the Bronx. Bosses from the ESU HQ at Flushing Meadows Park also headed toward Brooklyn, as did senior officers from 1 Police Plaza. A cop-shooting polarizes the force into one giant family, whose heart misses a beat: as every officer begins his or her shift, what they are thinking is "There but for the grace of God go I..." Upon hearing the news there isn't an officer in the department, whether he is testifying in a Manhattan courtroom or walking a beat at Rockaway Beach, who doesn't want to drop whatever he is doing and race over to lend a hand.

The shooting of Officer Cannon was one of those rare instances in the city when ESU units from all over New York respond. Lieutenant Greene, the first ESU supervisor on the scene, reached the outer perimeter of Frenchie's Cycle World fifteen

Sgt.Mike Mazza and Officer Dennis O'Connell from Floyd Bennet Field stand ready to deploy the ERV on Flatlands Avenue. On this occasion the armored carrier was not needed.

minutes after the initial call, and assumed immediate command. Officers from Seven-Truck, suited up, were covering the store with MP5s, Mini-14s and shotguns; reinforcements from Six-Truck and Eight-Truck provided additional manpower to secure the back and side exits; Transit Police ERU officers, with MP5s and heavy vests, joined in the task of securing the perimeter. Hundreds of other officers also rushed to the scene of the stand-off. Virtually the entire "6-9" was out in force, from patrolmen to plain-clothes detectives, as were uniformed members of the service from the nearby 63rd, 65th, 73rd and 75th Precincts. Officers, detectives and bosses from the Brooklyn South Task Force arrived on the scene, as did nearly all of Brooklyn's plain-clothes detectives, who were now helping out with crowd control and with co-ordination of the manpower and machinery making its way to Canarsie. Bosses of all ranks showed up in their dozens, including Chief of Department Louis Anemone, a charismatic and innovative commander, who donned flak vest and helmet and headed for the ESU Command Post. Two Aviation Unit helicopters flew overhead, and two others were fueled and ready to go.

By 4.36p.m., when Lt.Sobocienski made it to the scene, officers from ESU Five-Truck on Staten Island had arrived, as had officers from Nine-Truck in southern

Above In the tense moments prior to the apprehension of the three suspects, ESU and Hostage Negotiating Team personnel wait under the lights set up on one of the ESU trucks.

Below A suspect in Officer Cannon's shooting is driven away in a detective's sedan, on the first step in what may be a lifetime's journey through the criminal justice system. New York's death penalty, permitting the execution of cop-killers, was enacted only after Ray Cannon's death.

Queens, and Sgt.Paul Hargrove's squad from Ten-Truck in northern Queens along with their Remote Mobile Investigator; Two-Truck, all the way from Harlem, had also responded with their RMI, and Sgt. John Boesch and his A-Team had come from their base in Queens in their CAT car. Units had also come in from Floyd Bennet Field, including observers and snipers who trained their Remington M-24 rifles through the store windows already peppered with 9mm holes from the fire-fight minutes before. Even the armored ERV was ferried to Canarsie on its flatbed transport. All ESU officers were eager to help out, and the plea of "What'd'ya'need?" was heard everywhere. There was no jockeying for position, no showboating, just the dedicated professionalism - ESU style - of a unit with a job to do. The NYPD had geared for war this warm Friday evening; the cop-shooters would not be allowed to escape.

A tense stand-off lasted for the next hour. A small fleet of Emergency Medical Service ambulances arrived on Flatlands Avenue, ready to establish a triage center and a casualty clearing procedure should additional gunfire result in casualties. The news media naturally arrived as well, flooding the area with television lights for "live" cut-ins to the afternoon news broadcasts. In a situation of this type ESU assumes command and control of the entire crime scene, their recommendations and requirements bypassing most rungs in the ladder of command. Lieutenant Greene was put in charge of seeking out the shooters. He established his CP, and assigned tasks to his entry and assault teams for any prolonged search inside the shopping plaza - inside the stores of the complex, on their rooftops, and inside their basements and crawl spaces. Nothing would be left to chance, and the officers would be exposed to no unnecessary risk. The robot RMIs were deployed as probes, as were dogs from the K9 unit. Officers from the Hostage Negotiating Team arrived, ready to try to talk the suspects out of a situation that could only end with them going to jail, or to the morgue.

Lieutenant Greene sent the dogs into the darkened basement, hoping that they would at least locate the perps, but without success. The supervisor had no choice - officers would have to go down and get them. This would be Seven-Truck's job. Officers readied the flashlights on their Glocks, Berettas and MP5s, and slowly made their way down the stairs, past the dead shooter's body, into the pitch-dark basement below. Slinking in and out of storage areas in a well-choreographed tac-

Below 6 December 1994, Smithtown, Long Island: a floral arrangement with Officer Cannon's badge number is readied for the funeral procession to St.Patrick's Cemetery.

This page Some of the more than 10,000 police officers from all over the country who showed respect and solidarity by attending Officer Cannon's funeral. Outside the church during the mass they release stress by mingling and talking with their own; note that their shields bear black mourning bands.

As his brother officers from the 69th Precinct carry Ray Cannon's coffin from the church to the waiting hearse 10,000 hands rise in final salute, and the NYPD Aviation Unit fly overhead in the missing man formation.

tical movement, they followed the golden rule of engagement: cover and conceal-ment. Each movement was covered by fellow officers, in such a manner that their entire bodies were not exposed; body bunkers were also carried - even though vests and helmets can stop most ordnance, perps have been known to use special high-penetration loads like Black Talon, capable of slicing through body armor.

Finally, at 5.20p.m., the three perps surrendered to the Seven-Truck officers. Under heavy guard, they were escorted out of the mini-mall by a Seven-Truck REP and driven to the 69th Precinct for questioning. By 6.30p.m. the last ESU squads, sobered by the afternoon's events, had left the scene to return to patrol and quar-ters in Brooklyn, Queens and Manhattan.

At 7.54p.m. Police Officer Raymond Cannon was pronounced dead on the oper-ating table; his wife of only three months had been flown from their home in Long Island to be by her husband's side. At a press conference outside Brookdale Hospital, Police Commissioner William Bratton announced that a hero had fallen in the line of duty. New York City Mayor Rudolph Giuliani, quoting a shaken Officer Murphy, simply said, "We just lost the best cop in the 69th Precinct."

*   *   *

Police Officer Raymond Cannon was laid to rest on 6 December 1994. His funeral was held at the St.Patrick's Roman Catholic Church in his hometown of Smithtown, Long Island - the same church where he had been married just three months earli-er. Over 10,000 police officers, from as far away as Philadelphia, Rhode Island, Canada and even California, made the pilgrimage to attend the ceremony, and they gathered outside the small church in an ocean of blue uniforms and white gloves that stretched as far as the eye could see.

The funerals of officers killed in the line of duty are deeply important occasions for the men and women in uniform; apart from providing an opportunity to pay respect, and to support the grieving family with a wall of blue, they are a psychological release for those attending, bolstering them against their own awakened fears with the sight of so many of their own gathered together. Black bands covered their shields, and many eyes filled with tears. The funeral was a vigil, and a final farewell to an officer who, in the words of his priest, "had died a violent death in a world striv-ing for peace." The small church could only hold 1,000 mourners, so the huge crowd of officers stood outside the red brick rectory, mingling and talking among them-selves. "Cop funerals are a terrific mechanism for release of tension," claimed one detective, whose cigarette was burning down to its filter; "it's a way to see old friends, and collectively salute an officer who died in the line of duty."

As the service came to an end the officers were brought to order by the NYPD Honor Guard and the mayor, police commissioner, governor and senior police chiefs

Mayor Rudolph Giuliani (center), Police Commissioner William Bratton and Governor-elect George Pataki (on the mayor's right), salute as Officer Cannon's body is carried from the church.

stood in line to salute the fallen officer one final time. Laura Cannon, overwhelmed by her loss, clutched a rose as she left the church. Cannon's brothers-in-arms hoisted the flag-draped coffin on their shoulders and carried it silently out to the waiting hearse. Ten thousand hands saluted, under the mesmerizing beat of NYPD helicopters passing overhead in the missing man's formation. Nearly 100 motorcycle officers from departments in New York and New Jersey escorted the funeral procession to St.Patrick's Cemetery. The cortege was escorted by the NYPD's Emerald Society Pipe and Drum Band, the heart-moving strains of *"Amazing Grace"* skirling out above the muffled beat of the drums.

On 7 March 1995, in an emotion-charged ceremony in the New York State capital of Albany, Governor George Pataki signed into law the death penalty; for the first time in eighteen years New York has the power to inflict capital punishment. Realizing the significance of a ceremony introducing to the books a law that would allow the state to execute cop killers, Governor Pataki signed his first name with the gold Cross pen which Officer Sean McDonald had carried in his gun belt, and his last name with a black ballpoint carried in the memo book of Officer Raymond Cannon on the night that he was killed. Laura Cannon wept as she clutched her husband's black leather memo book to her chest; Sean McDonald's widow Janet stared toward the heavens for strength, but in the end she too could not hold back the tears.

Above Members of NYPD's Emerald Society Pipe Band escorted Ray Cannon on his last journey, to the haunting notes of *"Amazing Grace"*.

Below The Blue Knights motorcycle club, made up of NYPD officers, make their way back to the city following Officer Cannon's funeral. Nearly a hundred motorcycle officers escorted the procession to the cemetery.

6

Tactical Training, ESU Style

When ESU personnel say that they are headed for "the Field", they mean Floyd Bennet Field in southern Brooklyn. Although this former World War II air defense station could be pressed into use as an emergency landing strip should a disaster befall JFK International Airport a few miles to the east, and is the primary launching pad for the choppers of the NYPD Aviation Unit, the Field is also the principal ESU equipment storage facility and training center. ESU's half of a massive, almost Victorian-looking red-brick hanger is a multi-faceted armory complete with weapons and vehicles, emergency care facilities - and hundreds of man-years of collective emergency experience. Much of ESU's most specialized equipment is based here: the M75 ERVs, the total containment truck, the containerized emergency rescue supplies, jet skis for water rescue, remote tactical trucks, and even two snowmobiles.

The Field is commanded by Lt.Glen Panazzolo, an officer considered a rising star in ESU, who is far more experienced than his youthful appearance suggests. Whenever a major job erupts on the city's streets, it is Lt.Panazzolo and his training cadre who bear the responsibility for rushing whatever is needed - perhaps tons of equipment, perhaps large, specialized vehicles - through the crowded and often double- and triple-parked city streets to wherever it is urgently awaited.

To most ESU officers the Field is much more than a storage facility, however; it is the Harvard of NYPD special operations skills, where the unit trains most of its officers for their tactical role. The Field is the domain of two wily and charismatic officers who know virtually everything that an ESU officer could conceivably need to learn about tactical operations. When they say they've seen it all, they really have.

ESU tactical training is the responsibility of Detective Denis Burke - who has 23 years on the job - and Officer Kris Brandt. Both men are lanky and confident veterans of some notorious stretches of Brooklyn. Burke and Brandt do not have to read *Soldier of Fortune* magazine for stories of gunfire and bloodshed, nor do they need to refer to a military manual to figure out the best way for a five-man squad to gain entry to a fortified crack den. They learned their skills on the streets, inside stairwells, and by being the first officers through the door. Whenever either one of them is asked about a particular scenario or situation, he will thoughtfully light up a cigarette and recall, "There was a time in the 7-5...," always referring to Brooklyn's most dangerous precinct. Having survived the job in the "7-5" is a rite of passage for any cop, but for officers now wearing ESU colors it is a badge of distinction. Few in the department know more about street tactics and weaponry than Detective Burke and Officer Brandt. In teaching their tactical classes they are joined by a small number of other instructors, including weapons specialists from the NYPD's firing range at Rodmen's Neck in the Bronx.

Since the advent of the "A-Team" these instructors receive a new class of students every few months - ten officers straight from the Trucks. Burke and Brandt aren't dealing with raw material; these officers are very far from rookies, most averaging eight years on the job and at least two years with ESU. They have made arrests, backed up precinct cops on gun runs and perp searches, and have accumulated their own share of tactical experience on hits. Yet experience can bring its own bad habits; and the A-Team training ensures the creation of a cohesive, co-ordinated team operating in near-perfect synchronization.

When the A-Team is formed, a sergeant is selected to command the unit and nine officers are picked off a volunteer sheet. In order not to deplete one Truck too badly at any given time the officers selected for the team come from virtually every squad in the city. Tasked with forging this new entity, Burke and Brandt must reintroduce their charges to the basics: "Room Entry 101," proper hand position on the body bunker, what not to do when hugging a wall, and all the rest. Most importantly, Burke, Brandt and Co. attempt to teach the officers the need to be smart and delib-

Left Detective Denis Burke, the ESU tactical training instructor, shares his experience with trainees at the open-air "Tac House" at Camp Smith.

Above and right Inside the Tac House in the hangar at Floyd Bennet Field. Officers move into position for a tactical entry drill; and on the word from Detective Burke, point man Officer Frank Camastro, from Three-Truck, bursts through the door carrying the body bunker and one of the red-painted training-purposes-only weapons used for these exercises.

Right Perched above the action, ESU tactical instructor Officer Kris Brandt watches the A-Team practising room entry techniques.

Below The team repeat the exercise, this time with the additional distraction of the choking cloud of smoke from a diversionary device.

Right Denis Burke reviews entry techniques with PO Ed Foley, Three-Truck, during A-Team training. Foley's holstered .38 revolver is an off-duty weapon; at "the Field" live firing is not carried out in the Tac House itself.

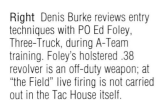

Above Camp Smith: against a scenic view of the Hudson River in fall sunshine, Officer John D'Allara, Two-Truck (right), prepares to rappel off the top of the 300ft. cliff. A week later he could very well be lowering himself down the side of a Harlem tenement during a tactical job.

erate, even in situations where fear and adrenalin reach alarming levels.

Once a tactical team goes through that door, there is a meticulous choreography of speed, finesse, power and movement that must be completed quickly and efficiently. There are, of course, obstacles that impede movement - furniture, booby-traps, pitbulls, and perps with guns. Anything impeding the officer's movement inside the enclosed space is an invitation to disaster - an exchange of gunfire, unnecessary discharge of a firearm, a police officer hurt or dead. Tactical training is designed to remove the "what ifs" and intangibles from the process of entry. If the perp takes a shot or does something stupid, so be it; but the ESU cops going in, with their minds focused on apprehending him, must know exactly what needs to be done, and must be completely confident in their abilities to meet the challenge.

"Unlike a military hostage-rescue unit," adds Denis Burke, "we are not at war with some terrorist group, and ESU has no such thing as 'acceptable losses.' We will not mount a job if there is definite risk to one of our officers. We have time, and we'll wait. What we do in training these teams is to make sure that officers don't fall victim to the unexpected. After all, you never know what's around the corner and behind the wall."

The ESU training facility at Floyd Bennet Field is inside the spacious old aircraft hanger. One section of this houses many of the unit's vehicles and much stored gear; there is also a mock-up helicopter hanging five storeys high, used during training of officers in rappelling and fast-roping from the NYPD Aviation Unit's seven choppers (two Bell-412SPs, four Bell 206B Jet Rangers, and one Bell 206L Long Ranger). Another section of the hanger holds the tactical classroom - a wooden mock-up of a perp's house, where officers perfect the skills needed to affect entry, search rooms, and take down perps - as well as a target firing range.

Standing high atop the wooden mock-up on a precarious catwalk, Det.Burke supervises as a team rehearse the proper method of entering through a door. In a narrow hallway nine men have assembled, all carrying the guns that a team would deploy on a job; two officers also carry the "body bunker" ballistic shields that can stop most handgun and shotgun loads. The mock-up is meant to give an impression of realism, and various furniture is placed around its rooms. In an actual hit the team would often have advance intelligence on the layout of the target from blueprints, and on the position of furniture from a marksman/observer perched across the street. For this exercise one instructor sits on a bed in the rear bedroom reading a copy of the *Daily News* - he's the bad guy. Hopping around the catwalk, Burke shouts, "Get ready, guys...Anyone in the house is a perp! Start when you're ready."

The shortest and fastest member of the team is the point man; he will enter first, carrying the body bunker and, if necessary, serving as a target to draw the bad guy's fire. The rest of the team will follow the point man throughout the apartment, constantly moving and never losing the momentum and flow of their entry. If the point man stops he bottles up everyone else, bunching the team into a big fat target for the bad guy. Each officer is also responsible for a particular room, which he must secure before allowing anyone else in.

The assault begins. An officer with an MP5 shouts "POLICE!" and kicks open the door; the point man enters, holding the 13lb. shield with one hand and aiming his 9mm automatic with the other. The other members of the team follow suit, searching the apartment for bad guys and anything else threatening. In the rear bedroom the instructor is spotted, and apprehended by a cop with an MP5. A secondary search is ordered, and any cranny or hiding place that might conceal a perp is carefully checked.

"Do it again," orders Det.Burke, "this time with a stun device." The officers reassemble outside the front door, with no sign of irritation; they are eager to do well, because the grade they are most concerned with is returning home in one piece after a job.

*   *   *

Contrary to what Hollywood and mass-market TV would have one believe, firepower is rarely used on the streets of the city; but officers obviously need to train in semi-realistic settings with live ammunition. Most live-fire training is carried out at the NYPD range at Rodmen's Neck; but the ESU's specialized tactical training is conducted twice and sometimes three times a year at Camp Smith, an Army post and training camp in upstate New York. Were it not for the National Guardsmen roaming the grounds in BDUs, and DEA agents practising rapid fire with their Glocks and SIGs, Camp Smith - surrounded by hills near the majestic Hudson River - might be

Left The famous cliff at Camp Smith, which all ESU officers have to negotiate before the end of the week's training; units which train here adorn the rockface with their emblems.

a suitable setting for a honeymoon resort or a hunting lodge. But it is here that ESU officers come to practice their rappelling and fast-rope techniques, courtesy of a 300-foot cliff and, weather permitting, helicopters flown up from the city. There is also a live-fire "TAC house" where forced entry skills can be honed up; VIP protection exercises are run here, using the CAT car, and recovery exercises with the ERV armored track.

The object of Camp Smith is to allow officers to refresh their individual skills in the basics of tactical work in a setting where they are separated from the squad-mates with whom they are used to working on a daily basis. In the week-long training periods carried out in the fall and spring officers are reintroduced to rope work, gunplay and tactical exercises that the narrow confines of Floyd Bennet Field cannot accommodate. In the week of tactical training all of ESU's 350 personnel will train at Camp Smith in shifts and cycles, ensuring that everyone goes through the courses without stripping the city's precincts of ESU back-up.

At the top of a 300-foot cliff overlooking the Hudson a class of officers engage in "rope work." In both rescue and tactical jobs ESU has been called upon to rappel down bridges and shafts, from apartment block roofs and helicopters. Some of the officers claim to love dangling a few hundred feet above the sidewalk; others are less enthusiastic. Yet when a barricaded perp is holding a family of four hostage inside a housing project, and the only way to get in with any element of surprise is to fast-rope down the side of a brick tenement, personal preferences come a poor second to getting the job done.

Camp Smith is easier than the streets. Here, down the tree-lined hill, the officers aren't wearing body armor, they don't have body bunkers dangling from their arms, and they aren't carrying MP5s or Ithaca 37s on slings. They can concentrate on the

Right and far right A green-capped instructor from the Rodmen's Neck range demonstrates the proper kneeling-firing position with the body bunker; and Officer James McVey, Two-Truck, hefts the 13lb. ballistic shield as he prepares to lead a team into the Tac House in a live firing drill.

cliff, on the ropes, and on getting down in one piece. It is an exercise in confidence-building, and the slide down the mountain at Camp Smith will be stored in each officer's mind the next time a worker is left dangling from a bridge, and the only way to get him down is to hook a line into him by fast-roping a few hundred feet above the water.

While one group of officers hang down the mountain, over on a parade ground another receives a class in VIP and dignitary protection with the CAT car; primarily, this involves bursting out of the vehicle with weapons at the ready should a motorcade be ambushed. The instructor, an officer from the Field, is concerned mainly with how long it takes the team to get out of the vehicle, adopt a proper firing position, and seek and acquire a target. In such a scenario the elapse of a few seconds will be of extreme importance, and the instructor stresses the need to reduce separate physical movements to a choreographed minimum.

At first the instructor insists that the officers practise these drills with imaginary guns; later in the day, after lunch and some climbing exercises, they'll display their skills with real weapons and live ammunition on the range. There are several live-fire ranges at Camp Smith, and the opportunity to expend large amounts of ammunition, in a variety of fixed and tactical settings, is of great importance. It allows the instructors to replicate specific scenarios, with ESU officers responding appropriately.

To teach the officers the A to Z of evacuations under fire the M75 ERV is brought up from Brooklyn on its flatbed transport. Many officers, including some with long experience, are somewhat daunted by the sight and racket of the blue armored personnel carrier bearing police markings. They are used to REPs and trucks, but not to a hulking steel box churning up the gravel with its tracks and belching a cloud of

Above and right Camp Smith: an instructor up from "the Field" shows off the interior and rear access doors of the hulking ERV (M75 armored personnel carrier) to an ESU squad about to practice the extrication of casualties under fire.

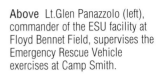

Above Lt.Glen Panazzolo (left), commander of the ESU facility at Floyd Bennet Field, supervises the Emergency Rescue Vehicle exercises at Camp Smith.

Left and below Even veteran ESU cops need special training to work safely in close proximity to the moving "tank" during officer recovery exercises. Outstretched arms indicate a safe distance from the tracks as the team prepare to give covering fire with Ruger Mini-14s and MP5s from behind the ERV. The officers wear the old-style ESU armor vest, with orange flaps for training purposes.

Above At the Camp Smith outdoor Tac House, PO Kris Brandt goes over the correct handling of a diversionary device.

exhaust smoke. The ERV training is handled by Lt.Panazzolo; it is his responsibility to get the officers used to walking alongside the ERV, and to show them what it feels like from the inside. He then initiates a series of scenarios illustrating jobs where the ERV might be called in, such as an officer down by his RMP under fire by a sniper. In one exercise Denis Burke, playing the sniper, pins down an officer riding in his patrol car with a volley of automatic fire. With one officer down and his partner calling in a desperate "10-13" over the radio, the ERV is summoned to extricate them. Moments later the roaring, squealing armored carrier appears from down the road.

The ERV needs to place itself between the sniper and the trapped officers; the cops inside the vehicle then provide covering fire while the patrolmen are brought to safety. When the ERV arrives its rear crew doors are thrust open, and an officer hurls out a purple smoke grenade, watching anxiously as a plume of colored smoke engulfs the entire area. Officers then race out of the "tank" and direct a hail of 5.56mm and 9mm fire in the sniper's direction, hopefully forcing him to take cover. Within a matter of seconds the trapped patrolmen are extricated and brought into the safety of the ERV, which slowly reverses out of the zone of danger.

The ERV exercises are valuable, though most officers hope that they'll never see this beast on the streets of the city: if they do, it will mean that there are civilians or officers down and under fire. The ERV has only been used in earnest on a few occasions. At the time of the Fall 1994 week at Camp Smith, the last time it had been brought out of its garage for real was in 1972 during the botched robbery of a sporting goods store by heavily armed militants, in which an ESU officer was killed. An ERV was deployed to the shooting of Police Officer Raymond Cannon in December 1994; and on 28 April 1995 both of the ESU's ERVs, together with a newly acquired Peacekeeper, were deployed to "The Winners" bar at Rockaway Boulevard and 112th Street in southern Queens, when an elderly man with a homicide conviction killed a bar patron and then shot at cops with a .380 handgun. According to Denis Burke, the ERV can be deployed from the Field in the southernmost tip of Brooklyn to any point in the city within an hour. Special routes that can handle the bulky vehicle on its trailer are marked on operational maps on file at ESU and Highway unit HQs. Many streets in the city are too narrow to accommodate it; others, above water mains and subway lines, might collapse under its brutal weight.

The true attraction at Camp Smith, however, is the outdoor TAC House. Unlike the equivalent exercises at Floyd Bennet Field, at Smith the officers honing their room entry skills aren't limited to using training guns painted red to simulate a real assault. When they go through the TAC House door at Camp Smith the weapons in their hands are real, locked and loaded. MP5 magazines can be emptied, and dozens of diversionary devices can be tossed inside without risking a cloud of blinding smoke building up inside the facility. It is at the outdoor TAC House that Det.Burke and PO Brandt can see how their charges handle moving through a multi-room mock-up while real 9mm rounds are being fired at close quarters.

As the officers unload a crate of ammunition and fill their banana-shaped MP5 clips, Burke and Brandt venture inside the TAC House and staple paper targets to the far end of the wood and canvas mock-up. There are five targets in all, and the paper silhouettes are clean - the officers can't claim later that any 9mm holes appearing outside the target area belong to someone else. A squad of five men is selected - POs, sergeants and lieutenants - and the tasks are divided between them. Detective Burke goes through the drill with the squad, telling them that this is nothing special, just a routine entry. The important aspect of the exercise is simple: unlike virtually all tactical scenarios that the officers will encounter on the streets, the

TAC House is entered with guns ablaze. It is meant to familiarize them with the sensation of live firing in an enclosed space - the noise, the smell, the ballistic sensations. It is also an exercise in target skills: "If you can't hit a paper target," says Officer Brandt, "then you shouldn't be aiming at real people on jobs."

As Kris Brandt peers into the TAC House through a slot cut out at a safe angle, far from the line of fire, Denis Burke signals the entry. The bunker man flings through the door and runs through the house to engage a target in the second room; he is followed by the rest of the squad, and the gunfire comes quickly. The whole assault lasts all of ten seconds, and after the order is given to stop firing Burke and Brandt survey the scene. "Don't aim so high," Burke tells one officer holding an MP5 with

Above and below The entry team assault the Tac House, engaging "perp targets" with accurate rapid fire from 9mm Berettas and Glocks and bursts from MP5s. The rooms of the mock "apartment" are cleared and secured within ten seconds under the critical eyes of the tactical instructors, and videos of the exercise will be reviewed later.

Above Harlem cops Lt.Bob Sobocienski, PO John D'Allara, PO James McVey and PO Dan Donnelly hone their 9mm skills on the Camp Smith range.

its barrel still smoking. "Ease into the target and position," Officer Brandt advises a cop holding his Glock tensely in both hands.

The squad will go through the motions at least a half dozen times before a new element is introduced - the diversionary device. Sometimes one will be thrown in, sometimes two. If they are to take advantage of a perp's momentary confusion officers have to be trained to ignore the loud blast and eye-popping flash. This time the officers have to locate, identify and engage their targets through a cloud of white smoke. "Looking good," Burke tells the squad, offering small suggestions to individual officers he may see encountering problems - in maintaining a good position while turning a corner, say, or spotting their target through the Plexiglass window in the body bunker.

"This time with a sniper," orders Burke. A sharpshooter takes his M-24 to a concealed position in the woods 100 yards away, and places his sights square on the head of a paper target in the second room of the TAC House. Officer Brandt will count to three, and the sniper will fire one round. The sniper's shot, meant to take down the perp, is the squad's invitation to go through the door; no diversionary device is needed. The squad enter the house and split in two. One two-man team race to the back room, and once firmly inside open fire on the paper targets. The point team have taken the first room, and empty their magazines in four-round bursts. Through the slot, Det.Burke and PO Brandt observe every small movement and make mental notes. They will critique any officer who holds his weapon sloppily, or who seems intimidated by the volume of live fire.

"It's hard telling an officer with ten years on the job and five years in ESU that he's doing something wrong," admits Kris Brandt, pushing his blue ear protectors down around his neck and starting to reload a Glock's fifteen-round magazine; "but they have to know the right way, if a disaster on the streets is to be avoided." Officers from the NYPD Technical and Research Unit have parked an REP next to the structure, with a video camera perched on the vehicle's roof. Every assault exercise will be taped, and reviewed later by the officers from the Field. Notes will be made and, hopefully, lessons learned and faults corrected.

On the outdoor range instructors from Rodmen's Neck, identified by their tan uniforms and green caps, supervise combat firing practice at close range with the officer's sidearm and the MP5. The NYPD's firearms instructors are perhaps the nation's finest, and can spot an error in stance or form in even the most experienced of officers. There are few mistakes to be pointed out. The head instructor, PO Ken LeGrow, orders the officers of one detail to holster their Glock Model 19s and, at the order commencing the exercise, to draw and fire five rounds in the prone position. A similar class is held for officers firing the MP5.

Some ESU officers claim to find the range of little practical value. "It's nice when you are plugging 9mm holes in the center of targets," says Det.Tony Sanpietro, a highly experienced member of the Eight-Truck squad; "but it doesn't help you with the Oh-S**ts." The "Oh-S**t" is the moment when an officer, walking a beat, is confronted by a perp with a gun. Without assuming the proper position taught on the range, without the benefit of ear protection, that officer must be able to pull out his weapon, hit the pavement in a vain attempt to seek cover, and then engage a perp who probably has a tactical advantage. Detective Sanpietro concedes that the training is necessary, however. "Even concert pianists must know how to play the scales, I guess."

After a full day of training, Det.Burke and PO Brandt decide to let the officers unwind and have some fun - day one has been tough, and Camp Smith lasts a full week. M-80 explosives are tossed onto the range, and for fifteen minutes the officers are allowed to shoot freely; the 9mm rounds ripping into the M-80s cause a series of loud and colorful blasts.

Over the course of the next few days, an NYPD Aviation Unit Bell-412SP will be brought in to add realism to the rappelling and tactical fast-roping exercises; and the TAC House will be assaulted a few hundred times more. In recent months an additional course has been added to the ESU tactical curriculum - operations *underground*. As the merger of the special police units develops ESU will take over all emergency jobs underground in the subway system from the Transit Police. Searching for an armed perp on rooftops or through alleyways is one thing; chasing him underground, on train tracks surrounded by the electric third rail, is a different story completely. At an abandoned subway station in Brooklyn, ESU officers are being taught what tactical life underground is all about in small and highly concentrated classes.

These tactical training courses are vitally necessary, and provide welcome breaks from the daily routine; but at heart, most ESU officers feel most at home inside their REPs, on the streets, where they know they are needed.

Below It takes tact and authority to convince ESU cops with years of street experience in some of the meanest precincts in the city that their tactical choreography may need adjustment; Det.Burke and PO Brandt bring both qualities to their work at the Tac House.

7

Sweet Justice For ESU

It was one of those typical winter nights in the Big Apple that drive the police crazy. A week of bone-chilling cold and twelve inches of snow had engulfed the city; at least cars couldn't be stolen - they were mostly buried under plowed mountains of slush. It was too damn cold for the average perp to be on the streets, and crime in the city had slowed down enough for most cops to catch up on their paperwork. But on Wednesday, 7 February 1995, the temperature climbed to a balmy 20(F); and New York's criminal element appeared to suffer from a mass outbreak of cabin fever.

Throughout the five boroughs during the 4-to-12 shift the SOD and precinct radios were hopping; city-wide, ESU's second squad would have barely enough time to grab some coffee or soup between calls that sent them back and forth through the slippery streets en route to job after job. In the Bronx, Three-Truck responded to a "10-13 shots fired," while Four-Truck had its hands full with a barricaded EDP. For Nine-Truck and Ten-Truck, Queens was busy with pin jobs and EDPs; and the REPs of Six-Truck, Seven-Truck and Eight-Truck were kept scurrying from precinct to precinct.

For One-Truck, the "Hollywood Truck," this evening would be spent on a divisional assignment which would also require back-up from Four-Truck and Eight-Truck. A divisional assignment can mean anything from a hit to something special; and tonight would indeed be something special - a taste of sweet justice. The ESU command center wouldn't say very much about the assignment, except that it was a prisoner escort involving a "Pakistani gentleman" who would be arriving at the South Street Heliport in lower Manhattan. Sergeant Karl Smith, the One-Truck supervisor recently arrived from the Housing Police's ERU, didn't think much of it; nor did Lt.Bob Sobocienski, the City North Supervisor for the evening who would be the boss on scene this frigid night. An escort could involve anyone from a mobster to an informant, and the TAC meeting, set for 19:30 hours at the heliport, would tell them all they needed to know.

The FDR Drive, the highway that runs along the east shore of Manhattan, had settled down by 7.30p.m.; rush hour traffic had eased down into a thin flow of cabs and buses, and only a handful of joggers braved the sub-zero wind-chill along the banks of the East River. An REP from each of the three Trucks participating in the "pickup" had arrived and were waiting for instructions. Inside the heliport's parking lot, however, the ESU officers were met by both NYPD officers from the Terrorism Task Force and agents from the FBI's New York office. This "Pakistani gentleman," the cops realized, was no ordinary felon or witness; this was a heavy duty group for an everyday perp. They soon found out that the visitor arriving later that evening was someone ESU had cause to remember: the escort would be securing one Ramzi Ahmed Yousef, who would be charged as the mastermind behind the 26 February 1993 bombing of the World Trade Center.

On that snowy February morning two years before, Ramzi Yousef had flown out under a false identity to Karachi, Pakistan, while his co-conspirators - the men who had brought the bomb across from New Jersey to the parking lot of the Vista Hotel - had returned home to watch the fruits of their labor on the news (and to await a knock on the door from the FBI.) The United States offered a $2,000,000 reward for information leading to Yousef's arrest; but the Kuwaiti-born terrorist managed to stay free for almost two years, roaming the Asian hinterland from Iran to Baluchistan, Peshawar to Baghdad. Yousef was overconfident for a man with two million bucks on his head. He continued to operate on behalf of his masters: in March 1994 he was believed to be behind a failed attempt to bomb the Israeli embassy in Bangkok, and in January 1995 he was almost arrested by the Philippine police after plotting to assassinate Pope John Paul II in Manila. On Monday 6 February 1995 he entered Pakistan on a flight from Bangkok carrying a false passport. Pakistani authorities,

Left Outside, it's a cold February night; in Two-Truck's quarters, Officers Dan Donnelly and Vincent Martinez carry out routine maintenance on MP5s and Ruger Mini-14s.

alerted by a tip-off, followed him to a Holiday Inn in Islamabad where he was arrested carrying a suitcase full of explosives.

Turned over to FBI officials the next day, Ramzi Yousef was put on a military flight which landed on Wednesday morning at Newburgh Air Force Base in upstate New York. There, under tight security, he later boarded a Sikorsky S-76 chopper to fly to New York City, where he would be formally greeted at FBI headquarters at 26 Federal Plaza, and then driven the three blocks to his new home at the Manhattan Corrections Center.

As the department's primary force for dignitary protection and VIP security, the ESU is also responsible for safeguarding prisoners who may be at risk of getting whacked en route to arraignment. This evening ESU was to provide back-up. The FBI and the US Marshals Service were determined to keep Mr.Yousef in their grip at all times; Highway units would safeguard the route, and ESU would provide the tactical muscle.

For ESU officers who had been on the scene of the World Trade Center blast, the job promised to be deeply satisfying - but also a daunting task. "This is serious s**t," remarked a terse PO Bill Pieszak, Eight-Truck, as he removed his Kevlar vest from the REP and fastened his helmet; "they want this guy dead, and fast!" Pieszak, as experienced an E-man as they come, was not known for false bravado; with more than twelve years in ESU, he has taken part in some of the tensest and most dangerous operations in Brooklyn's recent history. In Eight-Truck's quarters, next to photos of a Truck fishing trip, hangs a framed cover of *New York Newsday* showing Bill Pieszak, suited up and cradling his rifle, escorting into custody one Larry "Crack-Head" Davis - a reputed crack dealer and alleged murderer, who had shot five cops who went to arrest him. Now, however, Bill Pieszak seemed genuinely concerned, as did his partner, PO Jose LaPorte.

Both cradled their Ruger Mini-14s in their laps and had their windows rolled down, allowing the icy breeze to keep them alert and focused. The two other REPs, from One-Truck and Four-Truck, also stood at the ready. Lieutenant Sobocienski checked over the detail and returned to his red Crown Vic supervisor's car to suit up. Highway Unit officers, recognizable by their squatted hats and black leather jackets and boots, also checked over their gear and vehicles, making sure that the patrol car's Ithaca was loaded and pumped for action.

At 9.00p.m. a tug from the NYPD's Harbor Unit approached the heliport and played its searchlight over the ice-filled waters. An Aviation Unit Bell-412 swooped in from the north for one final aerial check. This was it: the Port Authority Sikorsky flew in along the river and made a quick, gentle approach to the windswept heliport. Mr.Yousef was not greeted on a red carpet by the mayor; but some of the US Marshals and FBI agents did smile as their shivering visitor was tucked into an FBI Crown Vic for the three-minute trip to the International Court House at the Jacob Javitz Federal Building, the New York base for the FBI and CIA.

The REP driven by PO Pieszak took the point, followed by POs Derek Dunston and Geoffrey Garner in the Four-Truck vehicle; behind them came the convoy of federal Crown Vics including Ramzi Yousef's ride, then the One-Truck REP, with the

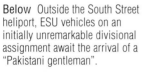

Below Outside the South Street heliport, ESU vehicles on an initially unremarkable divisional assignment await the arrival of a "Pakistani gentleman".

City North Supervisor car bringing up the rear. Highway units secured the route, ensuring that no wayward motorist would present a tactical dilemma to officers keyed up to meet a suicide attack by members of the Islamic Jihad. With lights flashing and sirens howling the escort convoy proceeded north along the South Street Viaduct to the Brooklyn Bridge off-ramp, north on to Centre Street, then west, then down Broadway for the turn into Duane Street and the secured underground garage of the federal facility. Highway units, the NYPD and federal officers had cordoned off much of the area to allow the convoy to bring its "package" in unhindered. Passers-by looked on in amazement. "It must be President Clinton!" shouted a Japanese tourist, excitedly snapping the shutter of her camera.

Outside the courthouse entrance on Duane Street shotgun-toting FBI guards secured the underground garage, as news crews - told of Yousef's arrival by a gleeful FBI, eager to announce to the whole world that they had got their man - interrupted local broadcasts with live feeds. Once the car carrying the prisoner had descended the ramp to an awaiting army of heavily armed FBI personnel, the ESU officers leapt out of their REPs and created a human perimeter of Kevlar helmets and MP5s. Eyes roamed over possible sniper perches in adjacent buildings, and weapons swayed towards any suspicious movement from the gathering crowd. The officers didn't know what to expect, but were poised for anything: Ramzi Yousef was a major league terrorist, who must have friends eager to see him silenced.

Lieutenant Sobocienski went inside the building to confer with his liaison from the NYPD-FBI Counter-Terrorism Task Force about stage two of the evening's activities: the package had, indeed, been delivered, but this was only his first stop. He was to be questioned here (and probably placed in a room opposite lots of federal agents high-fiving one another). Then, through the streets of a city alerted by the media, he would have to be transported three blocks to the Manhattan Corrections Center, where he would be just an underground tunnel away from the Federal Court House at Foley Square.

Ramzi Yousef spent nearly two hours at 26 Federal Plaza, while ESU spent the

Above The importance of this "package" is now clear. Lt.Sobocienski, CNS, and One-Truck's Sgt.Karl Smith (center) confer with Highway officers over details of the ESU escort for the car bringing Ramzi Yousef from the heliport to FBI headquarters.

WANTED BY THE FBI

AIDING & ABETTING; IMPORTATION, MANUFACTURE, DISTRIBUTION AND STORAGE OF EXPLOSIVE MATERIALS

RAMZI AHMED YOUSEF

DESCRIPTION

Date of birth: May 20,1967; Place of birth: Iraq (also claims United Arab Emirates); Height: 6'; Weight: 180 pounds; Build: medium; Hair: brown ; Eyes: brown; Complexion: olive; Sex: male; Race: white; Characteristics: usually clean shaven; Social Security Number Used: 136-94-3472 (invalid SSAN); Aliases: Ramzi Yousef Ahmad, Rasheed Yousef, Ramzi Ahmad Yousef,Kamal Abraham, Muhammud Azan, Ramzi Yousef, Rashid Rashid, Kamal Ibraham, Ramzi Yousef Ahmed, Abraham Kamal, Khurram Khan

CAUTION

YOUSEF ALLEGEDLY PARTICIPATED IN THE TERRORIST BOMBING OF THE WORLD TRADE CENTER, NEW YORK CITY, WHICH RESULTED IN SIX DEATHS, THE WOUNDING OF NUMEROUS INDIVIDUALS, AND THE SIGNIFICANT DE-STRUCTION OF PROPERTY AND COMMERCE. YOUSEF SHOULD BE CONSID-ERED ARMED AND EXTREMELY DANGEROUS.

April 1993

same length of time outside in the bone-chilling cold. If you were lucky enough to be standing near an REP's exhaust it was a mere -15(F) with the wind-chill - perhaps too cold for a terrorist strike? Perhaps just the right weather?... At 10:30p.m. Lt.Sobocienski emerged from the heated halls of federal justice and sought Sgt.Karl Smith. "They'll be bringing him out in a few minutes, let's get everything ready." The news media, eager to catch a shot of Yousef inside the FBI sedan for the 11.00p.m. news, had parked their vans outside the garage entrance on Duane Street, with satellite hook-ups on the vehicle roofs extended and raised. Once the motorcade started for the MCC a news truck, a cable or any other delaying obstacle could be just that chapter from Murphy's Law which gave a terrorist time to squeeze a trigger. "Sorry, guys, you're going to have to move it to the side," Sobocienski insisted to the nerve-frayed producers and reporters; "you gotta keep the street clear."

Officers Dunston and Garner, and One-Truck Officers Charles Dell'Accio and Kenneth Winkler, gunned the engines of their REPs. Inside the One-Truck supervisor's car Sgt.Smith and PO Brown made visual contact with Lt.Sobocienski. Officers Pieszak and LaPorte, the mobile point-men, were waiting on the corner of Lafayette, in position to secure the motorcade with their Mini-14s. They wanted to get the show over with and head back to Brooklyn; it was time to get the bastard into his cell.

At 11:00p.m., just in time to make the evening news, the sunken garage doors swung slowly open, and the FBI officers standing watch outside shifted their eyes from the garage to the surrounding streets and buildings - one hand for the portable radio, the other for the automatic weapon. The One-Truck REP went first, followed by the FBI cars, the One-Truck supervisor's RMP, the Four-Truck REP, and Lt.Sobocienski's car. The ride to the MCC took all of 90 seconds: the convoy crossed Lafayette, Centre Street, then veered left down Pearl toward a secure, well-lit reception by heavily armed FBI agents and US Marshals. Ramzi Yousef was driven straight through to his new home while the ESU officers emerged from their vehicles, weapons in hand, to secure this last leg of the operation. This was any terrorist's last chance to reach the prisoner for tonight, and nobody on the job wanted this victory to end in a long and bloody mess through relaxing too soon.

When the doors of the facility were sealed shut the FBI agents lowered their CAR-15s and entered the building, as did the US Marshals. A sergeant from the NYPD-FBI Joint Counter-Terrorism Task Force thanked Sgt.Smith and Lt.Sobocienski for the back-up. ESU's work was over - almost; but not before Sobocienski had gathered his officers for the brief review he insists upon, no matter how big or small the job. Mistakes should be pointed out while they are still fresh in the mind; and praise for a job well done loses its impact if given too long after the fact. There was nothing to downplay tonight; the men had done well, and the mission was completed.

It was near the end of the shift on a cold and unforgiving New York night. The Eight-Truck REP returned to Brooklyn, the Four-Truck vehicle headed back to "Ice Station Zebra" in the Bronx, and Sgt.Smith and company returned to quarters for the night's paperwork, one final cup of coffee, and a few more minutes with an ear turned to the SOD radio. Just in case.

Lieutenant Sobocienski headed back to SOD HQ in Flushing Meadow Park, hoping that he'd seen the last of Ramzi Ahmed Yousef and any of the other suspects implicated in the World Trade Center bombing. It was an optimistic wish. Yousef's arrival in New York City coincided with the opening arguments in the trial of blind Egyptian cleric Sheikh Abdel Rahman and several of his followers. At the time of this book's writing, the court proceedings promise to last as long as sixteen months, and their potential for associated violence cannot be discounted.

Left "Wanted" flyer on Ramzi Ahmed Yousef, who evaded capture for almost exactly two years after the World Trade Center bombing, despite a two million dollar reward. ESU's part in the process of his return to face justice was highly satisfying for officers who had been on the scene of the blast.

Above Officer Derek Dunston, Four-Truck, braces his Mini-14 as he plays a watchful part in providing tactical back-up for the last leg of Yousef's journey from a hotel room in Islamabad to a monitored cell at the Manhattan Corrections Center.

Sweet Justice For ESU

Left An FBI agent armed with a shotgun helps secure the area. News crews were alerted to the fugitive's arrival early in the operation, increasing ESU's concerns over a possible terrorist attempt to free or silence the suspect on their watch.

Right A snatched photo of Ramzi Yousef's departure, well covered inside an FBI car, from the secured parking garage at 26 Federal Plaza for the last leg of his trip to the MCC.

Left Like the ESU officers, members of the US Marshals Service spent hours in the freezing night securing the stops along Yousef's journey, and hoping for a quiet and uneventful prisoner transfer.

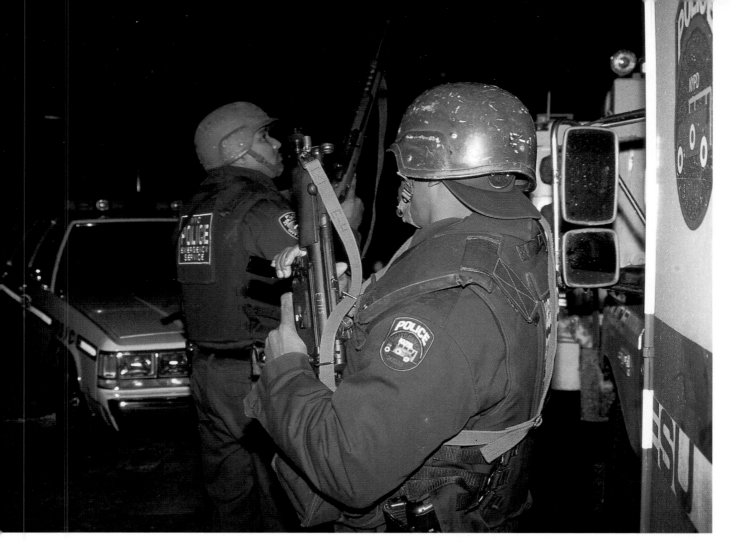

Above Weapons at the ready, Four-Truck Officers Derek Dunston and Geoffrey Garner keep a close watch on surrounding rooftops during the final phase of ESU's role in securing Yousef's delivery to the MCC.

Right A job well done: an FBI agent closes the gate behind Ramzi Yousef at the MCC, where he would spend the night before arraignment before a judge the next morning.

8

Dress, Decorations and Dedication

Readers of this book might notice that ESU officers throughout these pages are wearing two different sets of uniforms. This is not because they are from separate Trucks, or members of the Housing Police Emergency Rescue Unit assigned to ESU. In October 1995, in celebration of the NYPD's 150th anniversary, the department will be changing its uniform from the dark royal blue trousers and light blue work shirt to a dark navy blue uniform, reminiscent of that worn by cops in the golden age of the force during the 1940s to 1960s.

ESU in one sense pioneered this change. In an effort to provide its officers with a more visible on-scene presence ESU began switching to a dark blue uniform several years ago, following the World Trade Center operation when some ESU officers were mistaken for firemen. Their change to the new uniform, with reflective identification patches front and back, was engineered by Lt.George Shanley.

The decision to change the department's uniforms was made after extensive research and, for the first time in the NYPD's history, distribution of a questionnaire to the rank-and-file. Commissioner Bratton (who several years ago, as chief of the New York Transit Police, initiated a change of uniform to boost morale) knew that officers do a better job when they feel pride in the uniform they wear. The decision on a replacement uniform was made by the officers: a committee was selected and a representative chosen from each of the major NYPD units. ESU's representative was Lt.Richard Greene, a sharp dresser with pre-departmental experience in the clothing industry. For ESU, it was decided to have a large reflective patch on the back of the uniform (easier to spot during major jobs), a smaller reflective patch above the left breast pocket, and a nametape and badge number above the right breast pocket.

The reader might also notice that many of the ESU officers featured in these photographs, especially those still wearing the old uniforms with their shields worn on the outside, have been highly decorated. Since so many ESU officers have decorations there was some discontent over uniform changes which prevented awards for valor and service being displayed in association with the shield. ESU people are nothing if not practical, however, and appreciate that badges and ribbon bars tended to get snagged or torn off during rescue operations, and tactical assignments when the heavy vest was thrown on.

As for medals, individual members of the service may be awarded departmental recognition (medals) in the following grades:

Departmental Medal of Honor Awarded annually to a member who intelligently and in line of police duty distinguishes himself by the performance of an act of gallantry and valor at imminent personal hazard to life with knowledge of the risk, above and beyond the call of duty.

Police Combat Cross Awarded for the successful performance of an act of extraordinary heroism while engaged in personal combat with an armed adversary at imminent personal hazard to life in the intelligent performance of duty.

Medal for Valor Awarded for an act of outstanding personal bravery intelligently performed in line of duty at imminent personal hazard to life under circumstances evincing a disregard of personal consequences, or for conspicuous excellence in service to the community.

Police Memorial Award Awarded to next of kin of a uniformed member of the service accidentally killed, on or off duty, while performing official duty at scene of incidents such as aircraft disasters, drownings, heart attacks resulting from pursuits, auto accidents, fires, electrocutions, etc. Presented at annual Medal Day Ceremony.

Honorable Mention (A) Awarded for an act of extraordinary bravery intelligently performed in line of duty at imminent and personal danger to life, or (B) Awarded for extraordinary initiative contributing to substantial improvement in Community Policing/Community Quality of Life.

Exceptional Merit (A) Awarded for an act of bravery intelligently performed involving personal risk to life, or (B) Awarded for an act involving: (1) Exemplary performance which substantially improves the quality of life in neighborhoods or communities through creative problem-solving ideas, techniques or skills; and (2) Exemplary performance and consistent progress in implementing meaningful, significant improvements in rendering/securing community service or fostering police-community relations.

Commendations
Awarded for an act involving: (A) Grave personal danger in the intelligent performance of duty; (B) A highly creditable unusual police accomplishment; or (C) Awarded for a display of initiative in fostering innovative, valuable and successful Community Policing/Problem-Solving Programs.

Civilian Commendation Awarded to civilian members of the service for: (A) Exceptional work in connection with their assignment; (B) Excellence in service to the community; (C) Fostering community relations; and (D) Displaying initiative towards community problem-solving programs.

Meritorious Police Duty Awarded for: (A) An act of intelligent and valuable police service demonstrating special faithfulness or perseverance; (B) Highly creditable acts of police service over a period of time; (C) An act which demonstrates highly creditable integrity; and (D) A highly creditable accomplishment contributing to the improvement of Community Policing/Problem-Solving.

Excellent Police Duty Awarded for: (A) An intelligent act materially contributing to a valuable accomplishment; (B) Submission of a device or method adopted to increase efficiency in an administrative or tactical procedure; and (C) An intelligent accomplishment which promotes improved Community Policing/Problem-Solving.

The following awards are issued to NYPD units:

Unit Citation Unit Citations recognize outstanding performance by an entire unit in developing and implementing Community Policing goals and objectives or other highly creditable accomplishments over a substantial period of time (calendar year).

Police Commissioner's Personal Letter of Congratulations Awarded to units who do not otherwise qualify for a Unit Citation.

A uniformed member of the service may wear the prescribed breast bar or other authorized ribbons at all times while in uniform (except when wearing corresponding medals.) A member who has been awarded the Departmental Medal of Honor,

Police Combat Cross or Medal for Valor is required to wear the breast bar denoting the particular award in lieu of the Honorable Mention breast bar previously awarded for the same act.

*   *   *

On the street, however, it is impossible to measure at a glance the courage, compassion and sense of duty that each member of the ESU brings to the job every single day. On 5 January 1987 Police Officer Frank La Sala, One-Truck, was in quarters when a fire raged through a building adjacent to the 13th Precinct at 222 East 21st Street. Grabbing a small air pack, Officer La Sala raced into the burning building, where his efforts helped save the lives of more than a dozen people. He became trapped on a staircase engulfed by flame, and collapsed; firefighters found him unconscious and burned over 55 per cent of his body. Frank La Scala died of his injuries days later; he was 36 years old.

More than 4,000 police officers attended Officer La Sala's funeral, held at St.Patrick's Cathedral on Fifth Avenue. His body was borne atop the One-Truck truck to a dirge of bagpipes and drums. Inside the packed cathedral Cardinal O'Connor described the fallen ESU officer as a hero, and possibly a saint: "Greater love hath no man than this, that a man lay down his life for his friends." New York Mayor Edward I.Koch went further. Looking at the ESU officers saluting the coffin on the truck, he said "I think that every police officer who has given his life for this society is worthy of being called a saint."

At One-Truck's quarters a photograph of Officer La Sala's funeral is displayed proudly on a wall covered with commendations and descriptions of heroism in the line of duty. Each day, as the officers of ESU suit up and prepare to enter their "tactical mode" and "rescue mode," risking their lives so that others may be free from the threat of crime or from the pain of a crippling accident, they realize that their tour might end with injury or worse. They are all too aware that they could be shot or burned, run over or trapped. But they do the job anyway. The officers hope for the opportunity to play a role in saving a life, or taking a violent felon off the streets of their city. They get no extra hazard pay, no special recognition, no perks; just the satisfaction of being there when others need help - whether fellow officers or citizens. That is what being in ESU is all about.

The Author

SAMUEL M.KATZ was born in 1963 in New York City, where he still lives with his wife and child. Since 1984 he has pursued a career as a writer and journalist, specializing in the history of the Israel Defence Forces, and the war against international terrorism, on various aspects of which he has written more than ten books for British and American publishers. He has also contributed many articles to international publications and magazines in the USA, Britain, France, Germany, the Netherlands, Greece, Russia, Poland, the Czech Republic, Israel, South Africa, Australia, Japan, Taiwan, and Latin America. His works are among those selected by the United States Special Operations Command for a bibliography specially prepared for use by officers researching commando forces worldwide. He has also worked for the Discovery Channel in Bethesda, MD, as a writer and technical consultant on several documentary series.